Things I Need to Say to You

A Guidebook for Communicating

with Those You Love about Your ADD

Scott Robinson

Author photograph: Elizabeth Castle Lane

For Teri,

still

Also by Scott Robinson

The Beatles Guide to Love & Sex
To the Toppermost of the Poppermost:
      Exploring the Chart-Topping Hits of the Beatles
Rock Candy: The Beatles
The Quotable Beatles
YesTales: An Unauthorized Biography of
      Rock's Most Cosmic Band
Red Brains, Blue Brains: Neuroscience and Donald Trump
Really Great Things That I Didn't Say
The Heart of the Scots: Love, Sex and Romance in Scottish History
A.I. in Sci-Fi: Fictional Artificial Minds
      and the Real World Awaiting Them
Chasing the Enterprise:
      Achieving Star Trek's Vision of the Human Future
Uncle Scott's Treasury of Useless Knowledge
Uncle Scott's Treasury of Random Information
This Is What I'm Saying:
      Burdens of a Midwestern Suburban Polymath
My Work Here is Done!
      More Very Random Essays on Weighty Matters
I Think I'm Right in Saying That?
      The Intellectual Chaos Continues!
The Children of Babel: Essays on the Inherent Nature of
      Artificial Intelligence and Consciousness
HAL 9000: An Unauthorized Biography
Shadows of Shadows

Table of Contents

Introduction

Hi, I'm Scott. I'm an adult with Attention Deficit Disorder.

I say that not to establish an Alcoholics Anonymous tone, but to establish up front that I'm not a clinical expert in ADD. Though I have some training in neuroscience, I'm not a clinical anything; I'm a technologist, a teacher, and a science writer.

I'm also a son and a brother and a dad, in ascending order of importance. I'm divorced, and I'm a failed partner several times over. And that's to establish that what I can offer in the pages that follow is experience.

If you're reading this book, then you've almost certainly had some similar experiences as another adult with ADD, or you are the friend or partner of such a person, and have shared experiences with them that will resonate in places as thoughts unfold below.

A big part of my own experience includes loss of love and friendship that might have been avoided, had I been equipped to set realistic expectations. That's the real killer in the lives of people like us; we disappoint our friends, our bosses and our families because we fall below their expectations, again and again. If we are able to present ourselves in such a way as to help others to understand who we are and how we enter the world early on, we are giving them a gift – our best selves – and giving ourselves a greater chance of building a strong and healthy bond with them.

Too often, it's the opposite: not only do we fail to set expectations, we try to hide who we really are. We keep our ADD to ourselves, struggling (usually in vain) to manage it alone, and we present ourselves inauthentically, people-pleasing or shying away from substantive participation in the lives of those we care about, for fear of being found out.

The idea here, then, is to assemble an expectation-setting kit – go-to explanations of our ADD experience and behaviors and thoughts that might help in improving expectation-setting, leading to stronger, healthier, more consistent relationships. This book contains such a kit – things we can say to others to make clear what we can offer, if others see us as we really are. Where possible, I've included some hopefully-useful metaphors and analogies that may help others grasp what we're trying to explain.

(I should also make clear that these are not by any means all my own. I am a member of Uncommon Minds, a private Facebook community, and we came up with many of them together.)

These things that need saying aren't all about setting expectations; there are also some forward-looking offerings about the things the ADD adult can bring to a new friendship or relationship, offerings that can make that new connection not only strong but adventurous.

It's my profound hope that something easier make your path not only more tolerable, but more joyous.

TALKING ABOUT

ADD ITSELF

"There's a science to my brain!"

There are things ADD is, and there are things ADD isn't.

Even those of us who "have" ADD or "are" ADD or whatever don't always fully understand what it is and isn't. But any one of us who hopes to fully communicate this part of themselves to an intimate partner or friend must not only understand it well, but be able to share it effectively.

So let's talk about that. We'll lead off with ADHD coach Jessica McCabe:

> ## "ADHD is a terrible name for ADHD. It creates a lot of confusion. We don't have a deficit of attention! What we have trouble with is *regulating* our attention!"

Thom Hartmann, author of *The Edison Gene*, takes it a step further: not only is ADHD *not* a disorder, it's an essential set of skills that enabled humanity's survival in prehistoric times, giving rise to the "hunter-child" - the seeker/explorer who, in the millennia before the dawn of civilization, could seek out food for the tribe.

ADD is neither a deficit nor a disorder, in this view, but a magnificent benefit.

What's going on inside this benefit?

It turns out that ADD/ADHD isn't the result of bad parenting or video games or our atrocious modern diet; nor is it a mental disorder or "condition".

It's the expression of a handful of genes that we're born with, and which we pass on to some of our children. Variations of two of these genes – DRD2 and DRD4 – determine how our brains process the neurotransmitter *dopamine*.

Dopamine plays a vital role in... well, just about everything that goes on in our brains. It produces a signal, a kind of *ding!* that sounds in our heads, indicating satisfaction, 'rightness', or 'all is well!' This *ding!* is all over the map, where our nervous systems are concerned: it plays a role in executive function, in motor control, in learning; it is the underpinning of motivation and reward; it is essential to arousal and sexual gratification. We couldn't function as human beings without it.

That dopamine *ding*, upon which so much of our moment-to-moment existence depends, is more difficult to achieve in our ADD brains. Our variations of those genes mentioned above express as lower dopamine receptivity in our nervous systems; put another way, we have a harder time getting to the *ding!*

To get that *ding!*, that 'rightness' signal, we need more input from the environment; we scoop into the world with both hands, seeking the stimulation that takes us to satisfaction. Others achieve their *ding!* much more quickly and with much less input. And so, to them, we seem obsessive.

They can turn on the radio and get their *ding!*
We must write "Hey Jude" to get ours.
They can watch TV and get their *ding!*
We must paint "Starry Night" to get ours.
They can play a video game and get their *ding!*
We must build a computer to get ours.
And so on...

There's much more to say about how ADD works in our brains to produce the kinds of people we become, but that will follow. This particular bit of sharing can be summarized for a partner or friend like this:

"There's a lot of misunderstanding out there about what ADD is and how it works. It's not really a 'disorder', and people like me don't *lack* attention – we just have less control of where our attention goes. It's because we're born with some genes that motivate us to seek out the new-and-different, sometimes to the exclusion of matters that are important but unstimulating. ADD isn't something that's *wrong* with me, it's something that *right* about me in a

special way. It helps me see beautiful things
in the world that others might miss. I hope I
can show you how that happens, over time,
and share with you what I find!"

"ADD folks like me have been around a looong time!"

Since ADD arrives in our minds through our genes, it's been part of the human story for many millennia – far back in prehistory.

This makes sense. For early human tribes to survive the pressures of the Ice Age, as well as constant predation (we were cat food), a wide variety of cognitive styles needed to be present in every tribe, to boost the chances of group survival. Different kinds of problems call for different problem-solving approaches. And ADD is a problem-solving methodology in itself.

Imagine a Paleolithic tribe. Imagine that every member of the tribe has ADD.

Well, ADD is a *great* primitive skill, per Thom Hartmann; with our ability to scan the environment relentlessly, looking for change, seeking what's different, we'd have been excellent trackers – we could find the gazelle herd out there in the wild, and the tribe would have steak that night. So an all-ADD tribe would be terrific, right?

Wrong. Another essential survival skill for our ancestors was not getting eaten. And nighttime, when the large predators come out, was particularly dangerous. Our protection was fire, which terrifies animals. We know from ancient archaeological sites that our forebears camped around large fires, both to stay warm and to ward off the cats.

Who keeps the fire going at night? An ADD person? Ha ha.

Human survival depended on a diversity of cognitive style within every tribe.

To get some insight into this dynamic, I recently conducted a phone interview with two with Chuck and Roger, two young tribal Cro-Magnons in the early Upper Paleolithic, male members of a clan roaming Western Eurasia. They had lots to share about their careers, their tribe, and life as it used to be…

<u>MY INTERVIEW WITH CHUCK</u>

So, tell us a little about yourself. What do you do for the tribe?

     I'M A SHIFT LEADER ON THE HUNTER-GATHERER TEAM.

So you go out into the savanna and…

     TRACK DINNER AND FIND SIDE DISHES. MY TEAM LOVES A GOOD MAMMOTH AMBUSH. APART FROM THAT, WILD BOAR. THE OCCASIONAL REINDEER. I SOMETIMES PINCH-HIT WITH THE ROOTS-AND-BERRIES GANG.

That sounds a little dangerous. Do you consider your job risky?

     HELL, YES! POKE A 9-TON LEATHER BAG OF MUSCLE WITH A SHARP STICK ENOUGH TIMES AND HE GETS PISSED. FIVE OF MY HOMIES GOT TURNED INTO ROADKILL IN THE PAST YEAR ALONE.

What drew you to this line of work?

     SEE, IT'S IN THE DETAILS. WHEN I WAS A KID I WAS ALWAYS GOOD WITH PATTERN-FINDING GAMES – "SPOT THE HYENA," "WHERE DID LITTLE BROTHER POOP," THAT SORT OF THING. HAVING THAT KNACK COMES IN HANDY WHEN EVERYONE'S FEELING PECKISH AND IT'S RAINING LIKE HELL AND YOU HAVE TO FIGURE OUT WHERE ALL THE CARIBOU WENT.

What do you like best about it?

     WELL, THE SCENERY CHANGES, YOU KNOW? AND MARCHING BACK INTO CAMP WITH LOTS OF GOODIES INSPIRES… OH, LET'S SAY, 'GRATITUDE' AMONG SOME OF OUR MORE ATTRACTIVE CITIZENS.

Is there a downside to hunting and gathering?

> WELL, THE AFOREMENTIONED GETTING-TRAMPLED
> THING IS ALWAYS A CONCERN, BUT ALMOST AS BAD IS
> THE PROSPECT OF GETTING LOST AND NEVER
> RECONNECTING WITH THE CLAN. I MEAN, THIS ISN'T
> AN ENVIRONMENT THAT'S PARTICULARLY CONDUCIVE
> TO AUTONOMY.

Is there anything you'd rather be doing?

> SOMETIMES I FIND MYSELF HUMMING A CATCHY TUNE,
> AND I WONDER IF I PULL OFF A SET OR TWO AT
> CAMPFIRE.

How would others in the tribe describe you?

> I THINK YOU'D FIND I'M WELL-LIKED AMONG THE
> CLAN IN GENERAL. I'M QUICK WITH A HIGH-FIVE OR A
> ONE-LINER. SOMETIMES I GO TOO FAR, I SUPPOSE.
> GOOSING TRIBAL ELDERS. PANTSING THE FIRE-
> TENDER.

What are your political views?

> MY FRIENDS WOULD TELL YOU I'M A PROGRESSIVE
> LIBERAL, AND I CERTAINLY THINK THAT'S FAIR... BUT
> I'M LESS SANGUINE ABOUT RESOURCE ALLOCATION
> THEORY THAN MY PEERS. IT'S LESS A QUESTION OF
> OPTIMIZATION FOR THE SAKE OF EQUILIBRIUM, AND
> MORE A QUESTION OF HOW FAST A ROTTING
> MAMMOTH WILL DRAW A CROWD IF YOU DON'T STRIP
> IT AND EAT IT IN A HURRY.

What does 'progressive' entail, in your world?

> WELL, IT'S ALL ABOUT EATING, ISN'T IT? ICE AGE OR
> NO, THE WORLD IS BURSTING WITH FOOD – YOU JUST
> NEED TO GET OUT THERE AND GO AFTER IT. SO, WHEN I
> THINK 'PROGRESSIVE,' I THINK, 'ASS IN GEAR'...

Would you describe your tribe as a society?

> IT'S EASY TO BE CRITICAL, YOU KNOW? WE LACK THE OBVIOUS ADVANTAGES OF HOMICIDAL RAGE WE OBSERVE IN OUR SIMIAN COUSINS. AND SOME OTHER SPECIES WATCHING US MIGHT JUDGE, AND SAY WE HAVE WAYYYY TOO MUCH SEX.
>
> BUT IT'S ALWAYS BEEN MY FEELING THAT DESPITE OUR OBVIOUS PHYSICAL DISADVANTAGES, AS A SPECIES WE KICK SOME SERIOUS ASS.

MY INTERVIEW WITH ROGER

So, tell us a little about yourself. What do you do for the tribe?

> THIS.

This, meaning…?

> THIS. SITTING HERE, I MEAN. BY THE FIRE. IT IS MY JOB TO TEND THE FIRE. KEEP IT GOING THRU THE NIGHT.

To stay warm.

> TO STAY NOT DEAD. THE FIRE KEEPS FELIX AWAY.

Felix…

> BIG CATS. THE ONES THAT EAT US. WE CALL THEM FELIX. FELIXES. FELIX CAN SEE IN THE DARK, AND WE, YOU KNOW, CAN'T, BUT FELIX IS SCARED OF FIRE. SO MY JOB IS TO KEEP FELIX AWAY AT NIGHT.

How long have you been doing this job?

> ABOUT AN HOUR AND A HALF.

No, I mean, altogether. As a career.

> OH. SORRY. SINCE I WAS… AH… LET'S SEE… THREE
> YEARS OLD. NO, FOUR. NO, THREE. THREE.

What drew you to this line of work?

> WANTING TO NOT GET EATEN.

What do you like best about it?

> WELL, IT'S EASY ON THE BACK AND ON THE MIND, AND
> THE BENEFITS ARE GOOD. BUT THE HOURS TOTALLY
> SUCK.

Is there a downside to keeping Felix away?

> SEE, THE THING IS, YOU KNOW HE'S OUT THERE, SO
> YOU'RE ALWAYS KIND OF AWARE OF HIM. SO I'M
> ALWAYS SCANNING FOR HIM, ALWAYS A LITTLE BIT
> AFRAID.

Is there anything you'd rather be doing?

> I THINK I'D DO WELL IN THE FINANCIAL SECTOR.

How would others in the tribe describe you?

> THAT'S NOT AN EASY QUESTION. YOU HAVE TO
> UNDERSTAND THAT WE DON'T HAVE THE NUMBERS TO
> EFFECTIVELY SEGREGATE, THOUGH I CAN SEE AN
> UPSIDE. SOME OF THE YOUNG PEOPLE ARE
> BELLIGERENT, UNCOUTH. ONE OF THEM KEEPS
> PANTSING ME.

What are your political views?

> I LIKE TO THINK OF MYSELF AS SOCIALLY LIBERAL,
> BUT FISCALLY CONSERVATIVE.

What does 'conservative' entail, in your world?

> WELL, IT'S ALL ABOUT NOT GETTING EATEN, ISN'T IT?
> THE WORLD IS SCARY, AND NOT EVERYONE AROUND
> HERE HAS ENOUGH COMMON SENSE TO SEE
> THAT. SO WHEN I THINK 'CONSERVATIVE,' I THINK
> 'PEOPLE WHO PREFER TO NOT GET EATEN.'

Would you describe your tribe as a society?

> WELL, WE HAVE WAYYYYYY TOO MUCH SEX, IF YOU ASK
> ME. SOME OF OUR FEMALES ARE… IMMODEST AT TIMES. IT
> MAKES ME REALLY UNCOMFORTABLE. AND FREQUENTLY
> SELF-CONSCIOUS. LESS OF THAT, I THINK, AND MORE OF
> THE HOMICIDAL RAGE OF OUR SIMIAN COUSINS, AND I
> THINK WE'D SOMEDAY RULE THE WORLD…

Thank you for indulging me in a bit of fun there!

Back to business. It's important to understand that ADD isn't just a cool perspective from which to live modern life; it's an essential part of the human story. How do you present this to a partner or friend?

> "Did you know that some experts believe
> that people like me were an important part
> of prehistory? A person who has what we
> now call ADD would have been an excellent
> hunter-gatherer, an expert food-finder.
> When I first read that, I thought it was cool;
> when I thought about it some more, it made
> feel a little more special. I'm kind of proud
> of that legacy!"

"I'm in very good company!"

ADHD has a high profile right now. It is currently receiving more research attention than depression, OCD, PTSD or bipolar disorder. Consequently, there's plenty to read about it on the Internet – some of it accurate, some of it not.

But what we've all seen, and gratefully so, is more and more of our ADD peers coming out into the open. Celebrities, athletes, business people, creative artists – famous people from every domain of life have come forward and shared their ADD nature.

There are also a great many figures from history, both recent and not, whose writings and creations and biographies emit the telltale signs of ADD.

The point is this: those of us with ADD are in very good company:

From History: Socrates. Da Vinci. Newton. Michelangelo. Pasteur. Van Gogh.

Leaders/Thinkers: JFK. Abraham Lincoln. Winston Churchill. Dwight Eisenhower. James Carville. Henry Ford. George S. Patton.

Innovators: Stephen Hawking. Frank Lloyd Wright. Jean-Jacques Rousseau.

Scientists/Inventors: Thomas Edison. Alexander Graham Bell. Ben Franklin. The Wright Brothers.

Billionaires: Bill Gates. Richard Branson.

Writers: Agatha Christie. Mark Twain. Katherine Ellison. Virginia Wolf. Robert Frost.

Athletes: Michael Phelps. Michael Jordan. Terry Bradshaw. Babe Ruth. Pete Rose.

Celebrities: Steven Spielberg. Walt Disney. Stevie Wonder. Jack Nicholson. Erin Brockovich. Will Smith. Woody Harrelson. Liv Tyler. Justin Timberlake. Britney Spears. Channing Tatum. Adam Levine. Cher. Ben Stiller.

Comedians: Whoopi Goldberg. Howie Mandel. Jim Carrey. Robin Williams.

What do these people have in common? Most are innovators; most are highly creative; many are polymaths, competent across several domains; many are misfits, or were at some point in life. Most have reinvented themselves more than once. Some were game-changers.

And we have what they have: that special ingredient that has empowered them to enter the world through another doorway – to which we have a key. Tell your partner or friend about that key:

"Did you know that a great many famous people have ADD, just like me? Will Smith has it. So do Whoopi Goldberg and Jim Carrey. Athletes, too, like Michael Jordan. John F. Kennedy did, and Isaac Newton and Leonardo Da Vinci and Ben Franklin - lots of inventors, in fact, especially Thomas Edison. In fact, ADHD expert Thom Hartmann says ADD is a sign of 'The Edison Gene', a sign of a highly creative person. I may not be Thomas Edison, but I could be his fifth cousin twice removed!"

SHARING YOUR
ADD EXPERIENCE

Setting expectations

The goal is to set expectations – to communicate to a partner or friend what connection with us will be like.

That's no small ambition: our reality is so different from that of most people that it's easy for them to be thrown for a loop by our way-over-there actions and responses. Everyone's behavior ebbs and flows to some degree, but to those not like ourselves, what seems normal for us can seem extreme. It isn't, of course; it just seems that way to them because they are *expecting something else from us*. And the differences they will see become amplified, a bigger deal than they really are.

We can do a lot about this, by setting expectations up front. This brings their reactions to us back into the realm of the manageable.

A big part of that expectation-setting must come from letting them see the world through our eyes. When we provide them with our view from within, we help them to understand our differences in ways that transcend behavior alone. They see what we are seeing through the lens of our emotions about ourselves, about others, and the way we must respond to a world not made for us.

Sharing that part of ourselves isn't easy. But it's essential.

"I've spent my life in hiding – even from those I love."

There's much to cover in the pages ahead, and it all hangs together around some common truths. So it's best to put the biggest of those common truths out on the table right up front.

Very early in life – as early as grade school – an ADHD child will realize s/he is different from her peers. This realization can occur at the worst possible time in a child's development, at that delicate moment when s/he is beginning to learn social connection.

This delicate phase in the child's life is usually a haven of adult support and encouragement, a time of happy exploration and experimentation with making friends and developing bonds. Most kids learn how to connect, how to reveal and share themselves. They experience inclusion and the joy of tribe. They have successes, they make mistakes, they learn, they grow.

That's most kids. For the ADHD child, it's very different.

For the ADHD child, this delicate phase is a protracted disaster. It is a cauldron of disapproval from adults, rejection from other children, exclusion from the group. Being labeled. Feeling unwanted.

So we learn to hide it. We mimic behaviors that we know will make us acceptable and suppress our natural voice. We develop strategies for presenting ourselves in ways that will lead to inclusion; we become, to some degree, someone else – or, at best, a watered-down version of our real selves.

ADHD coach June Silny frames it like this:

> "Beneath my bubbly, exuberant exterior
> I hide a lifetime of anxiety, but people
> see a neatly-made bed, a promotion at
> work, dinner on the table, and children

who make it to school (just barely) on time. They see a competent, highly-functioning superwoman with a smile on her face. But behind that smile, I'm holding my breath or gritting my teeth almost all of the time – sure that my house of cards will fall at any moment. Thanks in large part to my ADHD, every task takes longer, feels harder, and wears me down in a way I could never explain. It's lonely, perplexing, and exhausting. This is what it's like to have ADHD."

This smiling façade takes its place alongside the other strategies, and ultimately it adds up to a life in hiding. The ADHD child grows up to be the woman June describes above, never quite free to be herself; the hiding becomes just a part of living. Failure in friendships, relationships, career, achieving personal goals – it all culminates in a message to self: you aren't worthy.

Or capable.

Or lovable.

...unless you present yourself as someone you really aren't. Someone more generally acceptable.

And so we fake it. We reveal only that part of ourselves we come to believe others will want around, and push down those feelings and expressions of ourselves that might not be understood or accepted.

And we become so used to this that we just come to accept it without thinking. We enable, and even approve of, our own emotional amputation. We become culpable.

This truncation of our real selves even extends to those we love the most – our best friends, our immediate family. They may know about our ADD, our impulsivity, our brownouts, our excesses – but that doesn't stop us from scrambling to hide them, just so we don't lose their love.

That's no way to live.

The problem becomes, how do we come out of the shadows and into more authentic relationships without alienating those we love?

There are two major components to solving that problem. The first is the management of expectations, which is the entire point of this book: if we want richer, more authentic relationships with those we care about, we must help them expect what will happen, rather than to be surprised by it – to make clear the differences between us up front, so they can gradually come to be treasured, rather than becoming burdensome.

The second problem is tougher. We, the ADD friend/partner, must do something that doesn't come easily at all: we must place our trust in the other, realizing that our trust may or may not be rewarded in the end. We must do what we've spent a lifetime avoiding – take a risk.

We have to let go of our façade, opening up about who we are, and presenting those parts of us that are different without shame or embarrassment. We have to say this is who I really am, and move through those disclosures about ourselves that follow in these pages. And we must do all of this within a framework of what may be unprecedented honesty and vulnerability.

If we undertake this difficult and frightening course, we will be rewarded in an important way, even if our efforts don't succeed, in the end, with a particular person: we will have presented ourselves in earnest, and the usual response is respect.

Respect for the ADD adult we actually are – that's worth embracing, no matter the outcome.

Here's a start...

"My ADD makes me different, and sometimes it's hard to feel different. To be honest, I've probably gone overboard, trying to fit in, most of my life. But I don't want to go overboard with you; I want to be myself, so that the things we do together and the conversations we have can be more real. I'm not always as authentic as I want to be – and I want to be, with you. If you'll let me share some things about myself, maybe it will help us enjoy our time together more deeply. Is that okay?"

Metaphors We Live By

Nothing connects one idea to another like a good metaphor.

In fact, metaphor – what Douglas Hofstadter has called *analogical thinking* – is the cornerstone of learning. When I realize that *this* is like *that*, my experiential knowledge of something I learned earlier boosts my understanding of something I've experienced more recently.

And so it is with ADD. Those who don't have it don't experience it; but we can boost their understanding of it by connecting it to something they *have* experienced.

You've probably heard this one. It's one of the most widely-used metaphors for describing the ADD experience:

"Having ADD is like watching TV while someone else has the remote and keeps randomly changing channels..."

~ADHD coach Brett Thornhill

This is a terrific metaphor, because it connects your experience to theirs; who hasn't sat next to a channel surfer and found it maddening? It also conveys to the non-ADD person the frustration that ADD adults often feel – an unfulfilled desire to take control, and the helplessness and irritation of not having it. When you're sitting next to the channel surfer and your eyes and ears are at their mercy, don't you want to just yank the damn remote right out of their hands? That's how it feels to be an ADD adult suffering from racing thoughts.

Harvard psychiatrist Edward Hallowell has made a career of explaining ADD to laypeople using metaphor and analogy. He has appeared on countless television shows, spreading a gospel of redemption to those who have ADD and understanding to those who don't. Here's one of his best:

> ## "ADHD is like having a Ferrari engine for a brain with bicycle brakes," he often says, capturing it exactly. Then he adds, "Strengthen the brakes and you have a champion."

Hallowell does indeed champion ADD adults. He told Carmine Gallo of *Forbes* magazine that "people with ADHD are the inventors and the innovators, the movers and the doers, the dreamers who built America."

With his Ferrari analogy, he does more than convey understanding; he removes stigma. He calls the Ferrari comparison "morally neutral," side-stepping the word "disorder" - ADHD, he says, is more trait than disability. Making it flourish as a trait is a matter of strengthening the brakes.

"We need to use more analogies in this field," Hallowell told *Forbes*. "With ADD, a list of symptoms doesn't show the power of the traits these people have—they are creative and imaginative. We're the people who colonized this country. Who would get on a boat in the 1600s and come over here? You'd have to be a visionary, a pioneer, a dreamer, and a risk-taker. That's why our gene pool is loaded with ADD. I see it as the American edge."

He's also very critical of how most people treat those with ADD, especially children. He's often used this one:

> ## "Telling someone with ADD to 'try harder' is like telling someone who's nearsighted to squint harder."

A great many terrific metaphors and analogies have emerged from laypeople with ADD. Here's a sampling from the website www.ADHDCollective.com, many of which originated on Quora:

"It's a horrible feeling – you're trapped inside your own head but not in control, kind of like the last scene in *Being John Malkovich*."

"It feels like my brain is understeering."[1]
(Colin Barrett)

"For me, it's like my brain is a computer with really low RAM."
"Sometimes I have this thing when (think of my brain as a computer) it's like someone tried to run a whole bunch of different programs all at once and the computer froze which really sucks because the only way to completely 'unfreeze' my brain is to 'restart' it (aka go to sleep)."
(Anonymous)

"It feels like my brain is a browser with way too many open tabs."
(Pat, on Quora)

---

[1] *Understeering* refers to power steering that isn't working. Have you ever tried to turn a steering wheel without power steering? It's like a gym workout.

"It feels like that scene in *Austin Powers* where the guy is just standing there for what seems like forever, staring at the steam roller, unable to get out of the way and it just runs him over."
(Lisa Perry)

"...like a roller coaster that never rests."
(Curtis Dickerson)

"Say you have a filing cabinet, and all the information is inside, but instead of alphabetical order, everything has been arranged every hour by a different person who did what made sense to them at the time. That's about how I feel my brain works."
(Valerie Fletcher)

Randall Munroe, a cartoonist who can be found at www.xkcd.com, created one called "Chasing Balloons" to convey the ADD experience – each balloon is labeled with a to-do task, and they are drifting every which way, and the person in the cartoon is trying to chase them all at once.

Rachel Binfold, on Quora, likened ADD to juggling on a unicycle:
"Every few years, I go to the local Renaissance festival," she wrote. "There's a guy there who juggles all kinds of random things – balls, swords, hats, fire, you name it. Then, he gets on a unicycle. Someone throws him each of the objects in turn and he starts juggling again.
"I'm sure he's practiced for years to do this, but when you watch him, he's shaking back and forth on the unicycle with an intense amount of

concentration. In just a few minutes, you can see the sweat start to bead on his brow from the effort. Even as a professional, he does actually drop things occasionally. It's not too long after that when the show ends and he gets to stop.

"Unfortunately, life never lets you stop juggling – there's work projects, home projects, kid's activities, household chores, personal life… Without ADHD (or any mental disorder, for that matter), you're standing on the stage juggling."

From there, Rachel compares ADD adults to non-ADD; ADD isn't the juggling, it's the unicycle:

"With adult ADHD, you're on the unicycle. Not only are you trying to juggle, but you also don't have a firm surface under your feet. It takes *lots* more concentration just to keep juggling because you've got the mental overhead of staying upright. Plus, you have way more balls, because your projects are broken up into smaller pieces. Plus, the balls are painted with super shiny colors. Your attention flits between the many balls because they're all coming at you at the same time and you can't just focus on one of them. If you happen to have a passion for red and deeply focus on those, you're going to drop something else.

"Not only are you trying to juggle, but you also don't have a firm surface under your feet. It takes *lots* more concentration just to keep juggling because you've got the mental overhead of staying upright."

She points out that, unlike the performance of the juggler, the ADD adult's unicycle is "invisible. No one gives you credit for the difficulty level of the juggling act. All they see are the number of dropped balls, not the effort it takes to keep them in the air. Because what matters in the adult world is the answer to the equation. You don't get partial credit for showing your work."

Finally, Rachel likens ADD medication to "training wheels on the unicycle. It takes the edge off the juggling act so that you can slow down and focus on each ball a little better."

And finally,

"Having ADHD/ADD is like having an iPhone loaded with apps and enabling notifications for all of them."

"If you did this on an iPhone," Kyle Pennell wrote, "you'd get overwhelmed with 'someone tagged you in X,' 'So and so checked in at X,' 'You've received a coupon for nearby y' notifications every couple of minutes. Only through practice and discipline are you actually able to turn those notifications off and actually get some function out of your tool. In this case, it's my mind."

That's enough to get you started, isn't it? Using metaphors and analogies that everyone who doesn't have ADD can easily relate to will hopefully lead them to understand you and what you go through a little better.
Can you think of some new ones?

COMMUNICATING WHO YOU ARE, WHO YOU ARE NOT

"I'm not lazy, I'm not insensitive, I'm not irresponsible!"

These are the great cultural clichés applied to both ADHD children and adults.

"You're lazy!" - because we aren't working on what we're supposed to be working on.

"You're insensitive!" - because we say the wrong thing or zone out on others.

"You're irresponsible!" - because we didn't get something done on time or didn't show up when we should have.

Almost all of us have been shamed with one or more of these accusations, usually frequently. The horror of this disconnect is that it starts when we are very young, and then never lets up. It drives us underground as we stumble into adulthood, forcing us into a life of pretense and cover-up, learning to make excuses and to suppress the parts of our personalities that contribute to our out-of-sync reality.

A new friend or partner, unprepared for the differences we harbor and the behaviors they will see, might come to these same off-base conclusions. We should address them early on.

"I'm not lazy!"

The ADD adult certainly is *not* lazy; we are engines of industry, often full of inspiration and dedication to a goal. We will, in fact, go way overboard in executing some tasks, becoming the opposite of lazy. Our issue is maintaining attention when the task is something that doesn't engage our industry; we certainly *want* to get it done, because it matters to someone else – but our dopamine receptors won't align. This needs to be explained to our partner or friend:

"My brain doesn't always cooperate, and I
need to explain that this is beyond my
control and not in accordance with my
wishes. There may be times when something
needs to get done, and I won't be getting it
done. I may need encouragement and
patience when that happens. I'll be open to
your nudges, and very accepting of your
help."

"I'm not insensitive!"

We are, if anything, oversensitive in just about every way! Our
emotional responses run deep, our empathy runs deep, and we feel things
with great intensity – we even feel the emotions of *others* with great
intensity!

Even so, because of our impulsivity and the speed of our thoughts –
combined with our brownouts – we can sometimes come off as
uninterested in others, or even rude.

It's entirely likely that this will happen with our partner or a close
friend, if it hasn't already. It's likely you've had this happen many times.
It's important to let the people in our lives know that it might, because
otherwise when it does, we look that much worse when our explanations
descend into excuse. Lead with something like this:

"Sometimes I zone out without
meaning to. It's not something I can really
control, and I don't want you take it
personally if it does. Just shake me a bit and
I'll snap out of it! And sometimes I might
interrupt you – that, too, is accidental. My
thoughts run fast and I blurt things out
impulsively. Feel free to point out when I do
this!"

Few things are tougher for an ADD adult than meeting deadlines. We have little sense of time, compared to others, and we easily fall away from our schedules. The result is often the loss of a job, the perpetual anger of our families and friends, and the cultivation of a reputation for unreliability.

In our hearts, we know this is unfair – but it's understandable, from their perspective. Right?

Much can be done about this. We have technology that can do a great deal to nudge us back on track, from cell phone notifications to reminders to the digital assistants, like Alexa, in our homes.

There's a darker aspect to this problem, however, and in these shadows, we are perhaps more culpable.

Often, we avoid some tasks or responsibilities altogether, because they intimidate or frighten us or fill us with dread, because we fear failing. And so we *do* fail, by not even trying.

We avoid some responsibilities altogether, and that never ends well, does it?

Both of these scenarios can and should be addressed:

"Sometimes I lose track of when I'm supposed to have something done. This makes my working life tougher, and it happens in my personal life, too. When I'm falling behind, your encouragement will help. I don't mean I need you to be my keeper or my alarm clock, but letting me know I've capable and that I've got this will be big motivators. And sometimes I might avoid something that frightens me – making me feel capable is even more important then. Thank you in advance!"

"I'm my own worst enemy!"

The world doles out many defeats to the ADD adult, perhaps more than can be counted.

ADD adults often dole out even more defeats to themselves.

Life with ADD is an unending parade of challenges, but often we set ourselves up to fail. It's not as simple as overreaching, biting off more than we can chew; we do plenty of that, of course, but the problem goes much deeper. Many times, we set out in pursuit of some success that's important to our career or to us personally, then sabotage our own efforts unconsciously, because in the back of our minds we feel we don't *deserve* to achieve our goal.

We get within reach of our goal and talk ourselves out of grasping it. We can't get there; we can't do it.

We're not good enough.

This kind of thinking has always been with us. The world has always sent us this negative message, back to early childhood – and we've been echoing it. Over the years, we develop a new voice – a voice that reflects our growing confidence, as we push back and achieve and hyperfocus our way to real competence and accomplishment – but even so, the two voices exist in our heads at once, often generating discord.

ADHD coach June Silny:

> "I teeter daily between self-confidence and self-doubt; never sure which will win. Some days, I jump into unknown situations with a confidence and clarity that shock even me. But inside a little voice is always telling me I'm just a child, an impostor of a grown-up. That

negative self-talk can nag me for days,
taunting me to push myself harder to
prove myself. And I usually succeed.
But, it's exhausting and painful to
reclaim my confidence again after that
monster called self-doubt begins
shouting, '*Who do you think you are?
You're getting in over your head. Stop
pretending to be someone you're not.*'"

If an ADHD coach still struggles with these two voices, what hope do we have?

For myself, I have to say that despite my confidence in my abilities today, which is pretty high, I do still hear that negative voice, pushing me to quit, to move on, to abandon my best efforts. Even when my confident voice wins, it's exhausting.

Here's where it's not only a good idea to share with a partner or friend that the second voice is there inside us, but that we could use a hand in drowning it out:

"Something you should know about me is
that I sometimes shoot myself in the foot! I
know we all do that sometimes, but I seem
to do it more than most. There are times
when I'm trying to get something done, and
I kind of give up on myself. I stop believing
I can do it. If you see something like that
happening, a word of encouragement would
be welcome! I know I need to develop the
self-encouragement to shut down that
giving-up thing altogether, but until I do,
your support is a big help!"

"I am most comfortable in clutter..."

And now for a bit of controversy.

Most of our ADD traits are, when carefully examined, positives that society shouldn't be trying to change in us. Most of those traits – deep-diving into projects, cultivating some excesses, indulging our desire to please - should remain untouched, simply presented differently or otherwise made easier to understand to others.

Our need for messes isn't one of them.

Most of us *love* clutter. We *love* it! We *love* stacks of things here and there. We love a room where there's a place for nothing and nothing has a place, other than *over there*.

This angers our parents, growing up. It annoys the coworkers whose orderly desks must sit alongside our chaotic ones. It vexes our partner or our roommate, who is forced unfairly to be uncomfortable so that we don't have to be.

At the same time, clutter *works* for us: it's a near-perfect visual metaphor for the wondrous diversity in our heads, the anything-can-happen dynamic of our thoughts, the surprise-at-our-fingertips nature of our emotions. We love the clutter of our rooms because it's a kind of passive permission to enjoy our minds.

That's almost impossible to get across to someone who knows how to put books back on a shelf.

My personal testimony here is pretty typical. For me, it's books.

As far back as my memory goes, my own clutter has been books. Sitting here typing, I can spin 360 degrees in my desk chair and see seven bookcases. All seven of them have additional books stacked at the top. There are three stacks of books on the floor to my left, two stacks on my right, and another stack on the coffee table.

And that's just one room. You should see the dining room table.

In fairness, I own more books than I have shelf space for at this particular time (and that's with 40 bookcases total in the house). Even so, it's a candid truth that I *love* my stacks of books. I couldn't do without them, and wouldn't have it any other way. As with us all, I look at my stacks of books and I see a reflection of my mind, and I'm giving it permission to be itself.

But then our problem resurfaces. It's easy for me to indulge myself here; my kids are grown, and they come and go, but other than that, I'm here by myself. There's no one else here to be annoyed or made uncomfortable by my clutter.

But that might change, any day. And then I have some hard choices to make.

...except that, we all know, it isn't any choice at all. A responsible adult, ADD or no, cultivates an environment that is welcoming to others. To do less is irresponsible and disrespectful.

The answer, I think, is middle ground. Yes, I need the visual metaphor and emotional comfort of clutter. But, as with all other indulgences, moderation is not only possible but preferable.

My next step will be to get my house in order, top to bottom – excepting a modest workspace that's mine alone, where books can pile up and notepads can be strewn about and I can feel like me when I'm getting things done.

The rest of my house can be a friendly, comfortable place I can share with those I love.

Does this all sound reasonable?

"I'm not sloppy – really, I'm not! Yes, my default organizational unit is the stack, but it's not like there are pizza boxes in the corners and dirty laundry on the furniture. The clutter I sometimes unleash isn't chaos – it's a kind of reassurance. It's a sneak peek into my brain, and it's kind of reassuring! I know that probably doesn't make much sense, but I promise it does. Even so, I don't want you to be uncomfortable – I want you to feel totally welcome in my space!

"I'll even welcome your suggestions about how I might organize the spaces we share. I'll get this under control, if you'll give me a little time, and I'll keep my clutter spot to myself. Fair enough?"

"I sometimes overthink things..."

This is so typical of ADD adults that it's a cliché. We are the world's leading over-thinkers.

It takes only a moment of contemplation to see why this is so. When faced with a situation that requires us to act, deciding how to act is a much bigger deal for us than most people, for two reasons: 1) we've blown it so often in the past by being impulsive that we don't fully trust ourselves, and 2) getting it right is so important, because we want to preserve the goodwill of anyone else involved, that there's some anxiety clouding our vision.

There's another factor, too, I think: when we're not acting impulsively, our novelty circuits are kicking in, and we get a little subconsciously creative: we are able to conceptualize a wide range of possible actions or responses – some of them useful, some of them extreme, some of them silly. And it takes a while to sort through them.

We have conversations with ourselves, as most people do, but ours go on endlessly. Again, no surprise there.

Here's where we might be jumping the tracks: most people think their thoughts and feel their feelings. But we're wired differently; we sometimes *think our feelings*.

- We feel something, and it isn't fun.
- We immediately jump to some explanation for the feeling, something we can bounce on and address, so that the feeling will go away.
- We start running open-throttle, evaluating competing explanations.
- We get lost.

We don't just do this when addressing a people problem. Any task or event in our lives has the potential to generate an uncomfortable feeling, so we overthink a wide range of things that may not require even a little bit of thought (and this never even occurs to us!).

We ADD adults, after a lifetime of anxiety and depression, is averse to simply *feeling our feelings*. It's horrifically uncomfortable, because we feel our emotions more strongly than most other people do.

The important thing here is to communicate this reality to your partner or friend, but there are a couple of things we can do about it that bear mention.

First, we can put our toe in the water and begin separating thoughts and feelings. This is very difficult, because of our racing minds, but it has to begin sometime. We need to give ourselves permission to feel, and to prepare ourselves for the cacophony that will surely nip at us when we make the attempt. It's best done in a tranquil place and moment, free of distraction, where comforts (anything from chocolate to a glass of wine) are close at hand. Quiet might be good.

Set a period of time for the exercise. Ten minutes, twenty, forty-five, whatever seems right. Set an alarm to bring back.

Then, just let yourself be sad. Or angry. Or whatever.

When narratives and explanations intrude, file them away for later reference. Just feel.

The second thing we can do is find someone to whom we can just speak the feelings. It need not the partner or friend we're trying to connect with – it can be an older friend or a family member or someone else we know who has ADD.

Let that person know ahead of time that you need to let some feelings out, but make clear that the point of the exercise is to avoid getting into thoughts about the feelings. They will keep you centered on your emotions and clear of explanations and narratives.

As for sharing this aspect of yourself,

"Do you ever overthink things? I guess we all do, sometimes. Me more than most. You'll notice this about me, if you haven't already. I have a tendency to overanalyze what people say, and overplan my responses. Part of this is insecurity that my ADD brings out. And part of it is that my thoughts and emotions kind of blend together sometimes, like food on my dinner plate! If you see this overthinking happening, there's a simple response that

will really help: just smile at me, and
squeeze my hand."

"I am all-in on many things..."

Hyperfocus – our ability to bring all of our resources to bear with extraordinary concentration, in the service of some awe-inspiring goal – has a side effect: it sweeps away barriers in other areas of our mind.

The ADD adult, given an area of interest and some hard-earned skill, goes all-in on that interest or skill. We create some self-indulgent wonder in our private world as a reward for surviving in the less-hospitable real world.

For some of us, it's collecting. For others, it may be cooking. It could be crafts, or restoring old automobiles, digital technology, gaming – you name it. We are world-class hobbyists.

One doesn't have to be ADD by any means to be an all-in hobbyist, of course, but it's very *natural* for us. It's an area where aspects of our ADD converge for a very positive result: it's quest for novelty plus hyperfocus plus impulsiveness plus nothing-is-ever-done. It's another permission we give ourselves to indulge those things that make us different.

And though we are by no means the only hobbyists around, we are certainly among the most excessive. We don't do things halfway – we go the distance like no one else.

An ADD adult will make every recipe in Julia Child's French cuisine cookbook in a year.[2]

An ADD adult will stay up all night learning a new programming language.

An ADD adult will read the Federalist Papers front to back.

An ADD adult will binge Doctor Who – the *original* Doctor Who.

An ADD adult will learn Mandarin, just for the hell of it.

---

[2] A New York woman named Julie Powell actually did this. Don't know if she's ADD or not.

To outsiders, these impulses may seem wasteful and pointless and even bizarre. But we know different: these impulses enrich us.

In a new relationship or friendship, however, this kind of all-in excess can't go unnoticed. So it's a good idea to set expectations, just so we don't come across the wrong way:

> "You may have noticed the 22 framed 1,500-piece jigsaw puzzles hanging on my apartment walls. Ha, ha. To be honest, I know it seems a little over-the-top, but in all honesty, *I* am a little over-the-top – and I like that about myself! When I really dig in and develop an interest in something, I go all-in: it's reassuring to me, when I find it so difficult to grab hold of life at other times. I hope you find this charming, or at least kind of fun – because it's who I am!"

THINGS YOU HAVE
TROUBLE DOING

"I have trouble saying 'No'..."

We ADD adults often don't know the word 'No'. We just cannot say it to save our lives.

The reason is clear. We have spent a lifetime starving for acceptance. Any request made of us is likely to draw a 'Yes!!!', however ill-advised, because it represents an opportunity to please another person, and thereby be accepted.

We are not, of course, the only people who have this problem. Many people who don't have ADD, but nonetheless must strive for acceptance, say 'Yes' too often. We can all agree, surely, on the consequences.

We overcommit. Saying Yes to everything leaves us no time to breathe. Or even sleep.

We often cannot deliver what we commit to. We say Yes because we can't say No, and find we've promised to do things we cannot do.

We can do the thing we agreed to do, but it won't be completed — because we're completion-challenged to begin with, but even more so when we've got too much on our plate.

We set ourselves up to fail, just so people will like us in the moment.

In the end, we wind up disappointing the person we said Yes to. The relationship is diminished, we are embarrassed, we feel a drop in both the connection and our self-esteem. We have failed someone, yet again.

This can't be fixed overnight. But it can be communicated up front to a partner or friend:

> "I'm sure you've known people before who
> had trouble saying No. Well, I'm one of
> those people. It's really difficult for me to
> turn someone down when they ask
> something of me. I'm not exactly a people-
> pleaser, and it's not my ego, thinking I can

do anything. It's more about being afraid to
let someone down by refusing their request.
I need to remember, in those moments, that
saying No is less of a letdown than saying
Yes and not delivering. I'm not asking
anything of you here; I'm just letting you
know I'm working on it."

"Hyperfocus or no, I have trouble finishing what I start..."

How many jobs have you lost?

If you're a typical ADD adult, this has happened. Maybe once, maybe a dozen times, but more likely than not, you've failed to perform in the workplace, to the point that your employer decided they could do without you.

That's one of the most horrible, soul-destroying feelings there is, isn't it?

It's one thing to have a friendship break, because friendships are subjective things; but to be dismissed from a job, where the to-do of the position is clearly defined and we openly failed to achieve it – that's not something that can be rationalized. It's sitting right there in front of us.

It's not just work in the office; it's *any* project that requires extended time and effort, from rearranging our closets to finishing our taxes to building a garage. We ADD adults are extremely completion-challenged. Getting to Done is perhaps our greatest single struggle.

Fixing it is the stuff of books, seminars, and online courses. Being an ADD adult and mastering project completion can (and should) be a lifetime undertaking. But part of that undertaking is sharing that reality with our partner or friend:

> "This isn't easy to talk about. You're going to rapidly notice, if you haven't already, that when I've undertaken some project, I struggle to get it completed. Yes, I'm able to focus intensely sometimes, and there are occasions when that focus gets me to the finish line. But not always, by a long shot. I

need you to know that when you see this
happening, pressuring me won't help (quite
the opposite); I *know* I'm running behind,
I *know* how much remains to be done. If you
want to help me along, the best thing you
can possibly do is see what I've
accomplished so far, and let me know what
you think. That will get my attention, focus
me on the project, and boost me toward
completing it. Thank you in advance!"

"I have trouble asking for help when I need it..."

Can I get an 'Amen' here?

If you're like me, you'd rather walk on Lego parts than ask for help when you need it. Once again, ADD adults are not, by far, the only kinds of people who have this trouble – but we are certainly among those who don't seek help when we are the ones who most need it.

We need help because our emotions are so intense.

We need help because we don't share the world's perspective.

We need help because our brains do not obey us.

We need help because we often do not believe in ourselves enough to get where we need to go.

And there are, of course, many other reasons. And the biggest of all may be this:

All our lives, we've been made to feel like a burden to others. And asking for help makes us feel exactly that: a burden.

But this isn't one that can just gradually improve over time, with our partner's awareness being sufficient as we go. This one needs urgent attention and cooperation, if the relationship is to have the better chance we want to create for it.

We need to begin asking for help – starting with our partner or friend.

That means we need to prepare for the occasional 'No'. That means we must reciprocate, and make ourselves as available to them as we want them to be to us. That means overcoming our fear that their support won't be as thorough and unconditional as we've idealized it to be in our hopeful imaginings.

And all of this needs to be said...

"I think you should know that I'm one of
those people who doesn't always ask for

help when they need it. Usually people like that are proud, and I want you to understand that's not me! I'm not proud, I'm just hesitant to be any kind of burden to other people. I know in my head that I'm not, but it *feels* that I might be, and I need to work through that feeling. You know that you can count on me to do my best when you need my help, and I may need to ask something from you from time to time. Is that okay?"

THINGS THAT
HAPPEN SUDDENLY

"I might suddenly go off on a tangent..."

Put racing thoughts together with impulsivity, and *BAM!* we're off to the races, pursuing a new thought that has no discernable connection to the old one. How often has this happened to you? You're sitting around with friends, all chatting about the ball game you all watched over the weekend, and suddenly you're into a story about the old car you fixed up in college when you scored a date with a cheerleader.

The origins of this tendency are obvious, and it's not such a tough one to address. Sheer practice will make us better at curbing this particular impulse.

The problem is this: when we give in to this impulse, we appear no different from those who hijack conversations. And intentional hijackers have motivations others frown upon: they're steering things toward their own agenda, or drawing attention to themselves, or have some other motivation that isn't going to sit well. We, of course, don't intend any of those things – but even so, we're setting ourselves up for disapproval when we go off on a tangent.

That's especially damaging in an intimate relationship. It's not only rude, and it not only raises suspicions about us – it makes the other person feel like they're not even really part of the conversation.

Staying focused in dialog, whether in a group or with our partner, is very important. We need to *always* be practicing impulse control. But that effort will be eased by sharing the problem:

> "I like that we can talk so easily about so
> many things. We have so much in common!
> Our conversations have been lively so far,
> don't you think? But be warned, sometimes

when we're talking about one thing, I might
sometimes go charging off, talking about
something else – because of my thing. When
that happens, don't hesitate to reel me back
in! I won't mind."

"Sometimes I will zone out on you."

I've had more than one relationship knocked off-kilter by moments of inattention in the midst of important communication. I believe most ADD adults have had such moments. Here's what usually happens:

- She sits me down on the couch to bring up her issue
- I listen and absorb what she's saying, nodding and smiling warmly
- Encouraged by my attention, she begins to open up emotionally as she continues
- Squirrel
- She keeps going, becoming vulnerable
- Squirrel
- Silence
- I realize she has asked me a question
- She demands an answer
- As I have done all my life, I fake it, rather than be honest about the squirrel; I get her to restate the question
- She restates the question
- Many squirrels
- She is insulted, because she was being vulnerable and I "don't care"
- Desperate, I say *exactly the wrong thing*
- Now she's pissed
- Desperate and frightened, I say another *exactly the wrong thing*
- Now she's *really* pissed
- Desperate, frightened, and now defensive, I say *the mother of all wrong things*
- She teaches me some new words
- I sleep in my car

Now it might not go exactly like this for you, but the gist is the same, right? Our brain channel gets changed in the middle of an important conversation, and we get pulled out of the moment.

But rather than rallying and getting back on point with our friend or partner, *we fake it.*

This faking starts when we are still young. We zone out when someone is sharing something very important, but we are too embarrassed to admit that we weren't paying attention, because admitting it might offend or hurt the other person – and other people who share important things with us are pretty scarce, we don't want to risk losing them. So we desperately try to reconstruct the conversation to some degree, all while babbling stupid things to stay in the game and cover our lapse. And we come off looking both uncaring and idiotic.

The thing is, after years and years of zone-outs and faking it, we have built a reflex: we pretend to be in the moment, after the fact, when we missed something important, and we don't fix it – all out of (bad) habit.

This is another one of those cases where we cannot help but see the other side. *Of course* our friend or partner will be hurt or offended if we seem unengaged or disinterested when they are trying to express something that's deeply important to them. *Of course* we come across as lame and ridiculous when we try to dog-paddle our way through it.

On the other hand, those of us on the ADD side of this dialog often can't do anything about the squirrel. Even when we've greatly improved our ability to hang in there, there are moments when the squirrel just jumps into our brain and starts dancing on the remote.

Thanks to CBT, this only happens to me now when I'm dog-tired, and both my brain and body are about out of juice.[3] The times it *has* happened, my fatigue made my handling of the moment all the more ineffective.

In the moment, this one is a lose-lose: fake it, and it's train wreck; admit the lapse, and you're risking anger and wrath (of these two, honesty is the healthier choice, of course).

So choose a moment before the moment, and smooth out the expectations of your partner or friend...

"Remember I told you about the 'remote' in
my head, how my brain sometimes switches
channels on its own? Well, that might
happen in a moment when we're talking

---

[3] A glass or two of wine really helps in such moments. Not.

about something serious, and I have a
tendency to pretend it didn't happen,
because it embarrasses me. When you sense
that I'm not hearing you, could you be
patient with me and realize that I care about
what you're saying, that I don't mean to
zone out? I want to hear from you."

"I might suddenly say something highly inappropriate without realizing it!"

This one is *big*.

It can happen anytime, anywhere, in any context. Our grasshopper minds are listening to others and racing at the same time. Our impulsivity grabs the nearest thought, and *BAM!* gives unfortunate voice to it.

In a group, that can mean saying something that might be hilarious in another context, or if phrased differently. It might mean saying something that isn't on-topic at all. It might mean saying something devastatingly inappropriate.

Our social filter has failed us, because our impulsivity caused us to bypass it.

"Oh, shit - I can't believe I said that!!!"

That's what we're saying inside, as the laughter that didn't occur settles around us.

And what do we do next? We fake it. We pretend we *meant* to say it, and act as if nothing is out of place. Someone jumps in with something new, to break the silence, and we pray to Zeus that we haven't turned red.

It's much, much worse in a one-on-one with our partner or a close friend. In that situation, it might be more than idle conversation going on. And inappropriate comments – humor, in particular – might be deeply offensive, impossible to circumvent. And our partner or friend is going to call us out.

And what do we do? We *still* try to fake it! We *still* try to cover the lapse and pretend we *meant* to say what we said.

"Well, I was just trying to lighten the mood..."

And, thereby, we make it much worse.

I was once a *master* of the Inappropriate Comment! I could bring group discussion to a crashing halt right out of the blue, regardless of topic or context. And I could alienate even the closest friend or partner with just the right touch of outlandish, offensive dismissal of an important matter – all by complete accident.

I overcame it through Cognitive Behavioral Therapy, which I believe to be a strong ADD adult go-to, when one is looking for relief and solutions. CBT is a methodology that trains us to step outside of thoughts that take us down the wrong path, allowing us to critically self-correct. It's like an alarm system in the brain that will warn of an approaching ADD moment. It isn't perfect, but it can boost our success level tremendously.

Because CBT won't save us every time, and we will still blurt out the wrong thing from time to time, our partner or friend should be prepped for it. Otherwise, any attempt to explain our comment after-the-fact will sound really lame – like a desperate excuse. Try something like this:

> "Remember how I told you my brain runs at high speed, all the time? That, combined with my impulsiveness, causes me to sometimes say the wrong thing. You know how sometimes you say something to someone and it just doesn't work? It can be embarrassing. It *really* embarrasses me, and I don't want to feel that way around you. Just like when I zone out, it isn't intentional, and I really don't want you to take it personally. Can you forgive me in advance, and point it out to me when it happens? I'll really appreciate your help in this."

THINGS ABOUT INTERACTING WITH OTHERS

"I may go dark for long periods of time..."

I have a superpower. You have a superpower. Most ADD adults have this same superpower.

It's our ability, after some indeterminate period of lackluster days and loosy-goosy underperformance, to seize upon a new idea or subject or creative thought and immediately pump oceans of adrenaline and enthusiasm into it. It's our capacity for surges of *over*performance, when we solve an unsolvable problem or undertake a daunting project or grab artistic inspiration and create a thing of staggering beauty.

We call our power *hyperfocus*, and for many of us, it's our proudest trait.

Hyperfocus is the other side of the attention coin, our compensation for all those times when we just can't offer what the world expects. It's that brief interregnum in our heads when *we* are in control, when we can seize the remote and keep the channel from changing while we do something amazing. It's us at our very best, when it comes to performance. We excel; we surpass ourselves; we exceed our peers.

Hyperfocus can sometimes bring us redemption in the eyes of those around us. It can boost our self-esteem tremendously, reminding us just how much we truly have to offer, when all is said and done. It should not define us, by any means; we all must see ourselves as more than what we can do. But it is certainly an important part of who we are.

Not long ago, I had a job with a health care company as a data scientist. My role was analytics – the mining of data for important hidden information that could produce value. The particular problem I was given to solve was formidable: I had to create a method of predicting the odds of a woman giving birth prematurely.

Much was at stake, because in each US state, hundreds of millions of dollars a year are spent dealing with the consequences of a pre-term birth. A normal, healthy birth today might cost between $8,000-$15,000; a pre-term birth, with weeks of neonatal intensive care and other through-the-roof expenses, can exceed $250,000. And that's before considering the human costs of a child who might never live a normal life, and the family that must adapt to accommodate such a child.

Finding a way to predict a pre-term birth, then, meant creating opportunities for early intervention to prevent it – to adapt the care the mother-to-be received to increase the chances of getting the baby to term.

The problem, I learned as I started researching it, was that no reliable method for predicting pre-term birth had ever been developed. This was completely new territory. And everyone around me was relying on me to solve it.

This really got my engine running. I *love* digging into a difficult problem, and this was a doozy! But more importantly, there was tremendous human consequence involved: solving this problem meant changing a great many lives for the better.

I started arriving at the office at 6 a.m., three hours before anyone else, so that I could work in peace and solitude. I started taking books and journal articles home at night. I took online courses to learn some tricky math. I made appointments with experts at the local university to bounce ideas off them. I spent upwards of $2,000 out of my own pocket to increase what I knew. I'm sure that to a casual outside observer I must have seemed obsessed.

In the end I succeeded, and it's one of my proudest professional accomplishments.

But it took its toll. The intensity of my hyperfocus was such that I had very little gas left in my engine at the end of every day. I was less present with my loved ones. I was less interested in our social circle. I was burning down to nothing. I didn't exactly shut everyone out, I managed to remain congenial – but I wasn't engaged.

During that time, I was with a supportive, encouraging partner. But not all partners and friends are so supportive when we ADD folks go dark, as our hyperfocus often makes us. We *need* our periods of hyperfocus, they're a natural channel for expressing ourselves and mustering those positive energies we carry within. We can't squander it or ignore it. But it does carry a cost.

So it's a good idea to have a mention of hyperfocus on the list of expectations dialogs:

> "A thing about me is that I sometimes get a
> lot of inspiration and energy for a project I

feel is important, and when that happens, I'll go all-in on it. When that happens, I might not be fully present for a while, or might at times seem altogether unavailable. It's important that you not take that personally; it's just the way I am, it's how I get important things done, and I'll be back soon. I will invite you into my process as far as I'm able, but don't be put off if I need some distance in order to complete my work. If you'll be patient with me, I hope to knock your socks off with what I can do!"

"I often run late..."

As ADD adults, we have a really crummy time sense. We wrestle with deadline and appointments and important dates all our lives. It seems like our minds are Swiss cheese, filled with data-leaking holes, when it comes to conforming to the world's clocks.

This is easy to understand. If there are a million things in the world that can't hold our attention, it stands to reason that the day and time those things are happening will hold our attention even less.

Worse, when we are hyperfocused, *nothing* can penetrate our minds; all our attention is going into whatever we're hyperfocused on, so there's nothing left to point us toward our appointment calendar.

There are, of course, more fixes for this today than ever before. We are surrounded by tech that can remind us of the clock, from our phones to Internet notifications to Alexa.

And asking your partner or friend for help with this issue is problematic: they, of course, will be on the dissing end of your lateness, yet it can't become their job to be your alarm clock.

Here's an alternative:

"You may have noticed – you have surely noticed! - that I am not the most punctual person on earth. This, too, is a consequence of my attention problems. Either the time I'm supposed to be somewhere slips out of my mind, or I'm so focused on something else that it doesn't make it to the surface. It's my problem to own, and it should never be your job to be my keeper in this area, but here's something that will help: when the thing to be remembered is important to us both – something we've planned to do together, for instance – I'm far more likely to be on time and present if you'll let me know you're looking forward to it, or to seeing me. When the thing to be remembered includes feeling valued, that's going to be a big boost!"

"I have an out-sized desire to please..."

This is one of those borderline traits that hovers between virtue and vice.

As an ADD adult, I love doing things that make other people happy. Part of this is the natural altruism and pro-social impulse we are all born with, rising to the surface, and part of it is – in all honesty – the sense of safety and security it gives me, knowing that this aspect of my personality brings me approval. Put the two together, and we have a clear understanding of our huge desire to please.

Because this trait swings both left and right, it's important to focus on what's motivating us when we are working on someone else's behalf: is it because we want to enjoy the happiness or satisfaction that our efforts will inspire in them, or is it because we're wanting to secure their approval?

The first is the purest of motives: making someone else happy for its own sake is a noble thing. And while doing nice things for others so that they will like us is perfectly human and not at all unacceptable, it's not nearly as good a motivation as the other.

We need to have this straight in our own minds. Just as importantly, we need to have it straight in our friend or partner's mind...

"Sometimes I come off as a people-pleaser, always doing things to make other people happy. To some degree, that's about me having trouble saying No – but the truth is, I do have a strong desire to please, and when you see me acting on it, I don't want it to come across the wrong way. I don't want to 'buy' anyone's love, and I don't just want their approval (although, to be honest, the approval of others does have a big effect on me). It makes me happy to see other people happy. Their happiness is important to me. *Your* happiness is important to me. And that what this particular side of me is about."

"If I interrupt you or talk over you, it's accidental."

ADD minds run at top speed, 24/7. Our minds *never* slow down, except for sleep and wine.

Consequently, we are world-class interrupters. We have a knack for listening to others and knowing where they're going with their thought before they do – and helpfully finishing it for them. Then there's our response to someone else's observation; before they're halfway through their comment, we've already gotten to the end and decided what we will contribute – and we do, while they're still talking.

Interrupting or talking over others is by no means restricted to ADD folks, of course; it's not exactly commonplace, but we observe it in others on a regular basis. Few, however, can compete with us; we are masters of the art.

In fairness to us, our powers of interruption have two sources, not one; it's not just the speed of our brains, it's that speed in combination with our impulsivity. There's little we can do about either. Through long and steady effort and practice, we can curb the impulse somewhat; but killing it altogether? Unlikely.

That's our cue to set an expectation:

> "I'm sure you've noticed that sometimes I
> interrupt you or talk over you. If I haven't
> already apologized, let me do it now. I need
> to let you know that it's not a bad habit or a
> lack of politeness training from my parents –
> it's part of my ADD thing. I'll try hard to do
> better, and I appreciate your patience. And

please, please, when I do it, point it out to me! I really want to get a handle on this."

"I might sometimes flake out on our plans..."

ADD adults can be world-class flakes. I speak as one!

I've flaked out on family, friends and coworkers hundreds of times over the years. Possibly thousands. We are big on bailing, aren't we?

The challenge here is pinning down *why*. Our flaking has so many causes!

- We're horrible with keeping track of time, and often just forget our commitments
- Our social anxiety flares up, and we just can't be around people for a while
- We're hyperfocused on something and can't be bothered
- We're pressured by rejection sensitivity and avoid a scheduled event out of wariness
- We're expected to somehow perform in front of others, and don't want to risk public failure

I'm certain we could easily come up with more.

Since there are so many causes for our not-showing-up, there's obviously no single fix. And even if we manage to improve at actually getting out the door and to our destination, those impulses that tried to hinder us are never going to die off; we're stuck with them.

Here's the thing: if we repeatedly don't turn up for our partner or close friend, they're going to go find another partner or close friend, and we'll become a memory.

"I have a really bad habit I need to be up-front about. There are times when I make plans and I don't follow through – I come up

with some excuse for not showing. I know
this is something that really irritates and
frustrates other people, and I regret it. The
thing is, there's no one reason why I do it –
there are several, and I need to work on each
of them. I want to work on this, and more
importantly, I don't want to frustrate or
irritate you! When I seem to be bailing on
something, could we talk it through? Please
press me for my real reasons. And maybe if
I'm resisting something I agreed to, if it's
possible, we could adapt our plans, rather
than scrapping them altogether? It's really
important to me that I get this right, and that
it not become a problem for us."

THINGS THAT COULD
HARM THE RELATIONSHIP

"I might idealize you..."

One thing is certain, concerning ADD adults: we do know how to idealize the people we're trying to love.

Non-ADD people often do the same, of course, but we have a special knack: when we're making a new friend or bonding with a new partner, our diminished sense of ourselves often nudges an augmented sense of them. We see them as better, more perfect, more worthy than they really are, and ourselves as less worthy than we really are.

We idealize them.

This tendency is often born of our endless cycle of hopelessness-hopefulness, when a relationship failure has been followed by an opportunity to succeed. Dysphoria greatly amplifies the sense of failure; our idealizing amplifies the potential success. We hypnotize ourselves into seeing more than is there.

It isn't really self-deception; it's more of a reflex, an accidental mis-evaluation that reflects our not-quite-right sense of self and others. We grew up believing we were less-than, and others more-than. The truth is that we're not perfect and neither are they.

The emerging problem is that when we enter a new friendship or relationship entranced by this illusion, we set ourselves up for disappointment and are being seriously unfair to the other. In our minds, we're not allowing them the freedom to be themselves. We're doing to them exactly what the world has done to us all these years – shooting them down with false expectations.

If a new relationship or friendship is going to have a chance of lasting, both we and they need to be real with ourselves and each other. The illusions generated by our idealizing work squarely against that.

Making them aware of this tendency will, hopefully, result in greater openness and candor from them, regarding who they are. They may be inspired to do some expectation-setting of their own, which is healthy and positive. The first move, however, is yours:

"A thing about me is that I sometimes see things through rose-colored glasses. I have idealized both people and relationships in the past. I don't want that to happen here. I want to be who I really am with you, and that means I need to let you be who you really are with me. If it seems like I'm too starry-eyed about anything, would you let me know?"

"I pretend, sometimes, about some things..."

Many of us grew up pretending.

We grew up struggling with impulse control, social awkwardness, an ocean of anxiety, and worked hard to hide it all, so that others wouldn't see what was going on with us and steer clear.

Some of us became very, very good at this kind of pretense.

Somewhere in our ADD logic, this made things better for us. We were rejected less. We were not as conspicuous. We succeeded in obscuring our flaws.

But in the long run, this hurt us more than it helped. When we fake it, we may get through the moment, but nothing ever really gets fixed. And things need to get fixed, if a new relationship or friendship is to truly become the one that works.

Here are some of the most common pretending scenarios:

"I pretend things are fine when they aren't..."

This is by far the biggest pretense we undertake. After a childhood of constant shame and belittlement, we learn to smile and shrug it off, just to stay in the world at all. Our dejection and disappointment, which we experience regularly, have no place on our faces.

As we become adults, we're expected to form our lives as others do, to create the order and structure that we see around us. But that's like being in a huge cooking class, watching everyone else prepare tasty meals with standard kitchen utensils and accoutrements, while we have to create the same meal with power tools. So we hide the dysfunction of our messy lives, put on a happy face, and deflect others from seeing how things really are.

We are, in short, master pretenders. It's a survival mechanism.

There's middle ground here. Our personal reality doesn't need to be shouted out to the world. It only needs to be made clear to those with whom we wish to communicate intimately – meaning we have to be genuine with those people. When things *aren't* fine – when we lose our job or we've lost someone we loved or something else has shaken up our lives – we need to be able to reach out honestly to those who can help. Something like this:

> "It won't surprise you that I'm pretty good at putting a good face on things. But sometimes, when things aren't good, I need to reach out and ask for help, and when that happens, the good face thing gets in the way. If I can ask you for help when I need it, I'll do my best to be transparent about the thing that's gone wrong. Is that okay?"

"I pretend I heard you when I didn't..."

This one is big enough that it has its own page (see "Sometimes I will zone out on you", page 52), but it falls squarely into the category of pretending. Someone's talking, we have a brownout, we miss something important, and then we pretend we didn't. We fake our way through, acting as if nothing is wrong, rather than risk causing them to think we found what they were saying unimportant.

"I pretend I didn't say that awkward/inappropriate thing when I did..."

This one likewise has its own page (see "I might suddenly say something highly inappropriate...", page 55). Our racing thoughts and impulsivity gang up on us, and we blurt out something stupid or irrelevant or offensive, because our social filters have been bypassed. And rather than try to explain our inappropriate words, we act like we *meant* to say that stupid thing. Of all ADD behavioral fails, this might be one of the most pointless.

Each of these pretenses, a solvable problem in itself, speaks to a larger, overarching one: inauthenticity. We ADD adults, as a matter of survival, often become inauthentic in the relationships that matter to us most. The individual behaviors need to be addressed, but the larger problem of being inauthentic likewise needs attention. Setting expectations here can not only smooth out future errors – it can boost a partner's or a friend's confidence in us and strengthen their resolve to help:

> "It's probably obvious that I've been embarrassed, many times, by my ADD mistakes. It's hard fitting in, when your brain often doesn't cooperate! The thing is, sometimes I try to cover up a mistake, just to avoid the embarrassment – and the covering-up is even worse. So I'm asking – can it be okay if I just make my mistakes? If you're patient about them, then I can be more myself with you. And that's what I really want!"

"I avoid confrontation like the plague!"

Here we find perhaps the greatest single convergence of ADD traits of all, combining to create a behavior that just sinks the ADD adult:

- A life in hiding
- Hypersensitivity
- Emotional intensity
- Anxiety
- Risk avoidance
- Insecurity/self-doubt
- Desire to please

Usually, by the time we reach adulthood, the ADD individual has concluded that conflict is always a no-win scenario. Resolution is usually very elusive, and the attempt is often as stressful as conflict itself.

Put another way, the cards are stacked against the ADD adult, when it comes to successful conflict management: so many things can go wrong, even when pursuing conflict constructively, that it's better to steer clear altogether.

No one who has spent many years in adulthood would fail to acknowledge the wrong-headedness of this idea, but we don't make this mistake with our heads – we make it with our feelings, which look at an approaching confrontation and shout, *"No way!"*

...and, almost inevitably, the avoidance of the conflict results in even greater problems: issues go unaddressed, becoming worse; eggshells accumulate, adding passive stress to every moment spent together; resentments form and begin to fester.

Eventually, confrontation is inevitable, and when it surfaces, it is now far worse than it would have been earlier.

No one can possibly blame us for feeling this way, or fail to see why confrontation feels so alien and toxic to us. After the lives we've lived, we would be perfectly happy to never argue with another human being again, *ever*. But that's just not how the world works.

The fix is slow, and requires close cooperation between partners (or friends). Learning to fight fair and fight well takes a long time, and is usually best handled with a coach of some kind – a therapist or counselor.

That's tomorrow's job. Today's task is to make this phobia clear, so that it can be (rightly) established as a relationship priority:

"This is a little hard to talk about, but I feel it's really important. In any relationship, things come up that need to be dealt with, and no two people always see eye-to-eye. Sometimes we disagree, and the disagreement can become a conflict. To be very honest, I'm not good at that. I'm so bad at it, in fact, that I work hard to avoid it. I know that's not a healthy thing to do, and that it doesn't solve anything – it only makes things worse in the long run. I do realize this about myself, however, and acknowledge the problem, and I'm embracing that as a starting point. The thing is, we can only learn how to work through conflict well together, and it will take some real effort. I'm willing to commit to it."

"I honestly don't even remember the argument!"

It was a Sunday afternoon in 2007. She and I were sitting on the couch, watching a movie on television, having just eaten a snacky lunch in the same spot. She was talking over the movie, and between the two, I wasn't catching much of either.

I can't tell you what the argument was about, but apparently I said something without thinking that really set her off – and when I tried to get her to disclose the details of the argument later, she only became angrier. That "pretending I didn't remember" only made it worse.

Over the next few weeks, this degenerated into a series of skirmishes and passive aggression, with the conflict itself never being addressed at all. In the end, a long-term relationship was in ruins – for no good reason.

To this day, I don't know what why she and I were arguing, or why we would come into conflict in the middle of a weekend movie on the couch. All the same, this same pattern has played out in my life twice since – and both times, I had no clue what started it, what it was about, what was said, or why I couldn't make clear that I couldn't discuss it if I didn't know what we were discussing.

Since that Sunday afternoon, more than a decade ago, I've done Cognitive Behavioral Therapy, and I am far better at attending partner dialog under overstimulating circumstances. I tend to only experience brownouts when it's late and/or I'm really fatigued, when mindfulness is next to impossible. All the same, it has happened – and I wasn't able to adequately convey that I had no clue what had happened, let alone discuss how to fix it.

At face value, it should be glaringly obvious: *I wasn't paying attention.* Memories don't form, or at best form very imperfectly, when attention is divided or absent. When we're listening to two conversations at the same time, do we remember either of them well? When watching television, are we able to also listen to a podcast? Attention and memory are inextricably bound together.

Schoolteachers understand this well. When two students attend class every day and the teacher presents the material clearly and thoroughly, and one student aces the following exam and the other one tanks, it's almost always because the second student *wasn't paying attention* – and thus did not remember the material that was taught.

When an ADD adult zones out and thus has fuzzy memory at best about some incident that really ticked off their partner, it's still their fault, because they weren't paying attention. But, of course, the ADD adult has little or no control over their own attention – *that's the entire point.*

Could she have turned the TV off and made certain I was refocused on her issue? Probably, but then, so could I, and as a matter of respect, it was more on me than on her to take that step – but too often, the ADD partner is too self-conscious to take such precautions. That's a weakness, and should be confronted (I'm working on it).

It's obvious that since the formation of memories requires attention, a deficit of attention will result in poor memory, but what exactly does that mean for the ADD adult? and what can be done about it?

German neuropsychologist Anselm Fuermaier and his team at the University of Groningen in the Netherlands did a series of studies on ADHD and its effects on memory:

"Memory functions of adults with ADHD," he wrote, "have been widely neglected in research for a long period of time. This is surprising, as many patients with ADHD report to often lose things, to not follow through on instructions or to be forgetful in daily activities. This is even more surprising considering that some of these behaviors are indicative of the presence of ADHD as outlined in international diagnostic criteria."

In other words, so deeply intertwined are ADHD and memory difficulties that the latter can become a red flag that uncovers the former.

Fuermaier's research determined that ADHD memory difficulties are different-in-kind from run-of-the-mill memory lapses. They are the result of executive function interruptions, which disrupt both the creation of a memory and its later retrieval:

"Even though adults with ADHD report to encounter considerable memory problems in daily life," Fuermaier reported, "these problems are most likely not caused by forgetfulness but may rather result from impairments of encoding (at the time when information is learned) and retrieval (at the time when stored information is recalled)."

More specifically, Fuermaier pointed to two essential components of memory: *prospective* memory, which is about performing an intended task in the immediate future (keeping appointments), and *source* memory, which refers to the information collected and stored at a particular time and place in the past. His research found that attention deficits affect both kinds of memory adversely.

"In the light of these results," he concluded, "we believe that the detrimental effect of executive dysfunctions on memory is so important that it should be considered in behavioral-based interventions which focus on planning as well as structuring and organizing information. Hence, memory functioning of adults with ADHD might be markedly improved by treating disorganization and planning deficits."

How does this help with the problem of partner conflict? Knowing what we now know about ADD's effects on our memories, it's easy to see that when a brownout triggers a conflict, memories of that argument aren't going to be well-formed; that's ironic, because it's a cascade of misfortune – the fight itself was accidental, and the fallout becomes worse, because of the memory fail.

In fairness to the angry partner, "I don't remember what we were fighting about!" *does* sound like an excuse; it sounds evasive, and the partner naturally feels that it's all being put on them. And that piles anger upon anger, making a mess-that-shouldn't-be a true crash-and-burn.

The thing to do is to present this truth about ADD and memory to your partner preemptively – or, if it's offered in hindsight, that a calm and unburdened moment be chosen to share it.

"Something you should know about me is that when I zone out, I often don't clearly remember what was said or what happened while I was zoned out. If that happens when we're talking – even when we might be arguing! - I might be looking right at you and still not having anything register. If you ask me later, I will tell you I really don't remember, and you can believe me. I hope you'll be patient with me and fill in the blanks, and I'll do my part to help resolve our disagreement."

"I feel rejection far more intensely than most people."

The last time I lost a relationship to ADD issues, I reflected long and hard about what I'd done wrong, and for the obvious reason – I had made the same mistakes I'd made in the past, and I wanted to stop making them once and for all.

One fact stood out: we'd had a big argument (about what, I still have no idea), and it was bad enough that she was furious with me; but the stand-out fact was that over the next few weeks, she gave me several opportunities to set things right – and I fumbled every one.

I kept reflecting, and thought farther back, to the two previous ADD relationship-enders. In both cases, my partner had given me multiple opportunities to fix things. One gave me *eight months* – and I *still* blew it.

Aha! I thought. Now we're onto something.

Parsing this realization, one thing stands out: the period of time following each rift was, to put it mildly, a terrible, non-stop anxiety storm. I can remember feeling the world crashing down around me, demolishing my peace of mind, my self-esteem, and my belief that I was even worthy of love. At work and with friends, I felt like I was sleep-walking; in interactions with my estranged partner, I must have seemed overbearing and desperate – and in each case, there came a point at which she said, "Enough!"

An anxiety storm – well, that was something I could work with. I started digging into the ADD research.

It didn't take long. It turns out there's something called *rejection-sensitive dysphoria.*

Rejection-sensitive dysphoria (from the Greek word *dysphoros,* meaning 'too difficult to bear') is a strong and sustained emotional response, akin to terror, occurring in the wake of rejection or abandonment.

Almost 100% of those adults with ADD have experienced dysphoria at one time or another, in the course of trying to maintain their relationships, and many have experienced it over and over.[4]

Per WebMD, the effects of this dysphoria are severe anxiety and diminished self-esteem, often accompanied by a pervasive feeling of hopelessness. Other symptoms include emotional outbursts, social discomfort, and contemplation of self-harm or suicide.

A person with dysphoria will tend to be easily embarrassed, more uncomfortable in their own skin than they already were. They will try to 'earn' their way back into the world through performance, and set impossibly high standards for themselves – and then punish themselves mercilessly when they fail to meet them.

These symptoms resemble those often seen in bipolar disorder, PTSD, OCD, and depression. Unlike the others, however, dysphoria is temporary; the anxiety storm passes after several weeks or months.

How does dysphoria come about? Put simply, it's the sudden surfacing of a vast reservoir of feelings that an ADD individual has accumulated since childhood. From an early age, they have been mocked or teased or otherwise made to feel excluded by other children, and have suffered endless disapproval from the adults in their lives, from teachers to camp counselors, and often within their own families. They have wrestled with the devastating effects of constantly being labeled 'trouble' or 'difficult'. By the time an ADD child finishes middle school, they have experienced *thousands* more negative comments and interactions than their non-ADD peers, from all sides – and this is *on top of* having far fewer friends, supportive adults and inclusive experiences in the first place. Is it any wonder that such a child grows to be an adult whose self-worth and sense of their own lovability are so easily knocked askew? Any rejection – even an imaginary one! - swiftly brings those many years of feeling inadequate right to the surface, upsetting the equilibrium of an already-precarious life.

A key thing to note about this dysphoria: when the literature emphasizes that it is far more severe than anxiety experienced by most people, that's no joke. Anxiety for a neurotypical person is unpleasant, to be sure, a thunderstorm with sheets of rain and bursts of lightning that sweep away peace of mind completely for a time; but dysphoria is Hurricane Katrina, lasting one or two orders of magnitude longer, leaving wreckage and devastation in its wake. Anxiety destroys situations; dysphoria destroys lives.

---

[4] It's interesting to note that the rejection or abandonment need not be real in order for RSD to be triggered; just the *perception* of rejection can set it in motion. Even an unanswered text can be a trigger.

In every ADD-driven breakup or falling-out I've experienced, intense dysphoria resulted. It persisted for weeks – in some cases, months. And in every case, the other person wasn't so much thrown by the ADD incident that put us at odds – they all offered to let me clean that part up. *It was the resulting dysphoria, not the ADD events themselves, that ended up destroying the relationship.*

Here's how it works:

An ADD relationship error occurs – angering our partner over some activity fail or inappropriate blurt or perceived insensitivity – but is eminently addressable. There's something tangible there to work with, and it's a doable thing to push through the anger or irritation and get to the root of the problem and fix it, working together. *Every* relationship includes that kind of work.

But dysphoria is different. It creates a gulf between us and the person we love, across which it's almost impossible to do any work on the relationship at all. On the ADD side, we are trapped in that growing anxiety hurricane, desperate to be pulled free. But it's a human constant that *anxiety begets anxiety*: when we are anxious, our anxiety spreads like wildfire, making the other person anxious. Our presence diminishes not only their interest in being around us, but their *ability* to be around us. And when we are reducing their own capacity by our mere presence, it's no surprise that they eventually don't want to be around us anymore.

Think about it: when did you ever have an anxiety-ridden person in your life and look forward to spending time with them? We do that kind of service for those we love, but only in small doses, and even though basic human decency moves us forward, the truth is that we usually dread it.

The thing is – unlike depression or OCD or bipolar disorder, dysphoria passes. And it passes fairly quickly, by comparison.

But *your partner doesn't know that*, if they don't know what dysphoria is! They are almost certainly thinking, *Geezus, is this how it's going to be from now on? No thanks!*

Nor do they realize that they usually have considerable power to dispel the dysphoria themselves, by helping their dysphoric partner to pass through the emotions that triggered it.

It's happened to me several times now. If I'd known about dysphoria to begin with, and shared that knowledge with my partner, I might never have gone through it at all.

More than one-third of adults with ADD say that rejection-sensitive dysphoria is the *most difficult part* of living with ADD (I'm one of them).

Have you felt that way? Has rejection by a partner or abandonment by a friend left you wondering how anyone could ever love you in the first place, and made you want to crawl into a hole? What did that episode do to your life?

Clearly, no one should ever have to go through such a thing. It's a good idea to go over this one with a friend or partner before it ever occurs. It's important to stress that RSD is something that almost all ADD individuals experience, not a feature of your own personality:

"There's a thing you should know about people like me, who have ADD: we sometimes feel a sense of rejection even when it isn't justified, and we can over-react. The truth is, during times like that I feel emotional pain more intense than I think I can even describe. It's called *dysphoria*, and it might cause me to act with poor judgment. I'm really not a drama queen, I just might seem like one! If I begin acting that way, please just sit me down and bring it to my attention, and if there's really something that needs work, we'll do that work together."

"*Dysphoria* is Greek for 'difficult to bear.' It's not that people with attention deficit disorder are wimps, or weak; it's that the emotional response hurts them much more than it does people without the condition. No one likes to be rejected, criticized, or fail. For people with RSD, these universal life experiences are much more severe than for neurotypical individuals. They are unbearable, and highly impairing.

"When this emotional response is internalized, it can imitate a full, major mood disorder complete with suicidal ideation. The sudden change from feeling perfectly fine to feeling intensely sad that results from RSD is often misdiagnosed as rapid cycling mood disorder."

~William Dodson, MD

THINGS YOU DON'T SAY
TO JUST ANYONE

"I'm more sensitive, in good ways and bad, than most people..."

Here's another double-edged sword.

Our heightened sense of our own emotions makes us very sensitive – sometimes highly empathetic, homing in precisely on the feelings of others and taking them in as our own, and sometimes highly overreactive, taking things too personally, allowing our own emotions too much freedom.

The point is clear here: the first is good, the other is not; the first is a tool for relationship-building, the other is a weapon we use on ourselves that harms our relationships.

The thing is, it's hard to have one without the other. The trick is to be more deliberate in our use of our sensitivity as an empathy generator, and practice better regulation of the emotions we allow to bubble up when we are taking something more personally than we should.

This is a tough self-disclosure to our partner or friend. It makes us vulnerable, and we naturally resist that sort of risk. But it's an unavoidable one:

"A thing about me is that I'm pretty good at picking up on other peoples' emotions. I like to think this makes me more understanding, a better friend. I hope I seem that way to you! On the other hand, as sensitive as I am to the feelings of others, I might be overly so when it comes to my own feelings. I may take things too personally sometimes. I'm working on that. If you see me seeming to

overreact to something you or someone else
says or does, please point it out to me?"

"My ADD wears me out – it leaves me exhausted."

This one is very important.

Any friend or partner, whether new or already in your life, needs to have an understanding about this aspect of ADD. It's exhausting.

We've already noted that living with ADD makes all tasks harder, all roads longer, all mountains higher. It truly is like juggling on a unicycle, and it leaves us with not much left.

On top of that, there's the emotional burden: we think we deserve extra credit, but instead we get extra criticism.

If we could slow our minds and take more control, we would. But we can't.

"The ADHD mind works a triple shift," said June Silny. "It never stops and it has no brakes. This makes me cranky sometimes. My emotions get out of whack, hard to control, and intense. I exaggerate and exasperate, and then I realize how poorly I behaved. My thoughts stand out like dominoes in formation, setting off a chain reaction. The movement only pauses while I sleep, if I can sleep with all those thoughts exploding in my head. My only relief comes from self-care. Quiet time is important. It's the only thing that gives my mind the space it needs to relax and recharge."

This captures it well, underscoring the energy cost of dealing with ADD while simultaneously getting things done. We simply burn up faster.

Much can be done about this. The self-care Silny speaks of is essential, and can bring great relief. But even this is something that must be carefully explained to a friend or partner:

"What's happening in my ADD is simple, under the hood: my thoughts *don't ever slow down.* I know that sounds a little goofy, but it's true. It's like when you're sitting in class and trying hard to follow what the teacher is saying? You can't do that all the time, right? Well, people like me don't have a choice – everything we do, day in and day out, is that intense. And on top of that, we don't always get to pick what we're paying attention to, either. I just want to let you know that this kind of wears me out. So when I seem wiped out and it's not obvious why, this is the reason. I just need to recharge."

THINGS YOU BRING
TO THE TABLE

Upsides

The preceding pages represent a great deal of expectation-setting. If you've shared these things with your friend/partner, you've covered a lot of important ground, in terms of what might happen as your connection proceeds and the relationship unfolds.

But most of what's above is offered as warning, sort of – look out for this bump in the road! These things should be said, of course, but it's easy to characterize them as your 'downsides'.

It's equally important to share some upsides.

Whatever sucks about having ADD, the truth we all know is that there's another side to the coin: we arc capable of wonders! We can do amazing things, and our hearts – though different! - are deep. We can bring great value to a relationship that will be unique, special, and unlike what our non-ADD peers might offer.

This should be said, and in ways that come across as hopeful, rather than boastful.

Here are some suggestions...

"I have a lot to offer this relationship!"

Say what you will about a lifetime of rejection and hiding and low self-esteem: it teaches us the immense value, the preciousness, of acceptance and connection. When you have less of those things than others, you learn to treasure them all the more, even if how to retain and nurture them is not always clear.

Out of adversity have many great stories emerged, and ours need not be any exception. Having lived very challenging lives, we've been changed in ways that have made us much stronger in areas we hardly think of. Our personalities have taken on features that we make take for granted, as necessities for just getting by in life. But those features, brought out into the light, can be tremendous assets when offered as gifts to someone we care for, rather than just survival tools.

Think of these traits as spiritual rewards, earned through our perseverance.

The list is long!

I am compassionate!

Our ADD adult tendency to absorb the emotions of others is born in our childhood, when we are studying the other children around us and the adults above us in a desperate bid to learn how to be accepted. We become unconscious experts in the emotions of others – and our own longing for connection often makes it inevitable that we would then soak those emotions up.

In describing this to one of my friends, I used the term "emotional sponge". She scolded me immediately, insisting that I reframe the idea. "You're not a 'sponge'!" she said (I think she was a little exasperated with me). "That's what we call 'empathy!'" She was right, of course.

The ADD adult is a natural empath, as a result of decades of intense attention paid to the feelings of others and our internal sensitivity to our own yearnings.

Caring deeply about others, causes, ideas – this is a tremendous asset in a relationship. It makes us safe, earnest, engaged, exuding a deeply human warmth. It means we can be counted on to listen, to be caring, to strive to understand.

All of that makes us very attractive as a potential partner or friend.

I am generous!

A child does not have to be ADHD in order to be generous. As early as 18 months, and even earlier, children demonstrate a natural inclination to share. This deteriorates somewhat when many children are put in the same space and territories spontaneously form, but the impulse to give is inborn [cite research ref].

Adults, of course, encourage the sharing impulse in children, and it usually isn't until adolescence that self-regulation of the impulse truly kicks in.

With an ADHD child, it sometimes never does.

Generosity, the child learns, is a path to approval and acceptance. This isn't to say that the ADHD child is concluding that love and acceptance can be bought; it is the extension of a desire that's already there, in the child's quest for connection. It is established early on that the giving of gifts carries emotions beyond the satisfying impulse that underlies sharing; it is the communication of how the child feels about others.

As the child becomes an adult, those feelings continue to feed into their thinking about others and their attempts at connection. Generosity is only one of several languages we use to express ourselves and connect, but for the ADD adult, it's a go-to. And generosity is a cornerstone of strong friendship and loving partnership.

I'm creative!

Almost by definition, an ADD adult is attracted to novelty. Our funky dopamine receptivity causes us to scoop stimulation out of the world with both hands, wherever we can. That attraction to novelty often manifests as creativity.

Indeed, it is difficult to list all the artists, writers, musicians, entertainers and other novelty-driven people who are likewise ADD adults. It's so common, it's a cultural cliché.

Creativity surfaces in many ways. Often, it's the artistic impulse; but it can just as easily emerge in a knack for cooking tasty and interesting meals, or doing a lively makeover of the family room. It can pop up in vacation planning and holiday events and the selection of birthday presents. There's no limit to the ways creativity can make itself know.

And all of them are a plus to a relationship.

I'm funny!

ADD adults are funny. Hilarious! You wouldn't guess that, but it's very often true.

On the face of it, it's hard to pin down why that would be – but a moment's thought reveals the answer: humor flourishes in adversity. It helps us cope, it keeps our outlook bright. It's not always there for us, it's sometimes elusive, but very often we are able to laugh at ourselves and the tough situations we've survived.

A pacesetter here is humorist Alison Larkin, who was adopted by a British family at birth. She later learned who her American birth parents were, tracked them down, and learned from them about the ADD in her genes.

It made total sense to her. The comedienne is also a novelist and public speaker, and has said that performing stand-up comedy for huge crowds is far easier than cleaning her kitchen or writing a letter.

Psychology Today affirms the positive impact of humor on relationships, citing a cross-culture study of 3,000 couples in five countries that demonstrated greater marital happiness among husbands and wives who had a humorous partner.

This is good news all around! It's is certainly, in many cases, a serendipitous benefit of ADD that can help smooth the way to eventual relationship success.

I'm spontaneous!

It's easy to frame this one as a polite substitute word for 'impulsive', but there's more to it, I think. Impulsivity involves little or no contemplation, which spontaneity is a positive emotional response to an impulse – and doing fun, unexpected things with a friend or partner outside of your normal routine can be thrilling, as well as healthy for the relationship.

"Spontaneity involves unpredictability and it heightens intensity and excitement in a relationship. Spontaneity is the opposite of routine," psychologist Kim Chronister told *Bustle*. "Intend to implement and maintain positive experiences of unpredictability by going above and beyond and getting out of your comfort zone by doing something or travelling somewhere, or buying tickets. A new activity is preferred because novelty spikes romantic feelings and overall attraction when it is experienced between partners."

Psychiatrist Tom Stevens added that spontaneity can keep both partners anchored in the relationship. "When one partner feels they know everything about the other partner, it can cause them to become disinterested," he said. "This is where spontaneity can be very helpful. Curiosity can be provoked by unpredictable circumstances, which are more likely to emerge with risk-taking."

ADD adults are impulsive, to be sure; but alongside that impulsivity exists a strong affinity for spontaneity that can be a joyous asset, helping pave the way to long-term relationship success.

I'm persistent!

Modern relationships are tough. We've created a culture that may be sensual and entertaining, but it isn't truly friendly to real intimacy and depth. It's hard work, making a relationship a safe and nurturing and satisfying place to live.

Our culture is equally unfriendly, if not more, to ADD individuals. The pressure to conform, the shame that gets heaped on those who don't meet expectations, the rejection of those who tire of us – all of this turns even a very ordinary life into very hard work.

And yet we've managed, haven't we? We're persistent. We hang in there. We tough it out.

That's what it takes to have a long and happy friendship or relationship these days. It's what it takes to live happily and productively with ADD. Persistence serves both very well.

I am resilient!

Beyond persistence – hanging in there – there's picking ourselves up off the mat when the world has knocked us down. It's happened all our lives, and we've learned to get back on our feet.

We're *resilient*. Our ADD lives have, necessarily, forced us to be. We struggle, we fall, *we bounce back*.

That's not something most of us ever even consider. But it's true.

And that's a wonderful quality to bring to a new friendship or relationship. Even the most successful couples experience times when their feet are yanked out from under them in the relationship. Responding well

in those times is as important as perseverance. And the ADD adult is a
veteran.

I am loyal!

This, too, we have spent a lifetime longing for from others. We want
their loyalty, because we know we will unwittingly test them, probably
repeatedly. We *need* their loyalty, to keep our connection strong when we
are not at our best.

Consequently, we have always been ready to offer that loyalty in return.
We have practiced it in our thoughts and displayed it when connections
took hold. We've been that person we want to have in our lives. We're
willing to stand alongside them, come what may, because we treasure them
above and beyond.

We've got this one.

"I'm a romantic inside!"

We ADD adults are natural romantics! People wouldn't guess that, but it's true.

Romance brings several of our ADD traits into positive convergence:

Novelty: Great romance is filled with surprises, with the new-and-different, with the unexpected; we ADD adults excel at those!

Empathy: Anticipating and receiving your partner's feelings, finding joy in them, and relishing those feelings that emerge in response are right in the ADD wheelhouse.

Passion: Hyperfocus and passion are deeply intertwined, and romance is hyperfocus by definition (it's probably the most common kind of hyperfocus that non-ADD adults can experience) - so ADD adults naturally shine here.

Put simply, ADD adults have all the necessary ingredients of true romantics.

On the other hand, fear of rejection and our natural reticence in social situations work against us. It's like having a pocketful of money and being afraid to drive to the store to spend it.

Putting ourselves out there requires some real courage; not letting ourselves get pulled off-track once we're on is also a consideration. Putting meaningful effort into romance can be a major plus in an ADD adult's quest for connection and a lasting relationship – but once again, it's important to not try to move the mountain alone:

> "I really love romance, and I'm enjoying all
> the things we're doing together! And the

best is yet to come. I'm excited about what's up ahead – and I'm going to be all-in on our plans and our trips and all the great stuff that's about to happen. I have lots that I want to bring to it all. And if it ever seems like I'm losing interest or not engaged, you can be certain it's just the ADD talking – my brain is needing a recharge. I'm loving every minute of it!"

"I'll do my part!"

One of the biggest issues in an ADD adult's marriage, or even space-sharing with a roommate, is division of labor. It's a huge contributor to relationship stress, and sits high on the list of grievances presented to the ADD partner when separation or divorce arrives.

Put simply, the ADD adult has trouble doing their share of chores. And this understandably creates friction that can burst into flame, torching domestic bliss on a regular basis.

"Broadly speaking, chores are typically left undone, poorly done or often put on the back burner unless there's a sense of urgency," says psychotherapist/ADHD coach Terry Matlen. This is more than laundry or taking out the trash; ADD adults often forget to pay bills on time, to return important phone calls, or to do essential paperwork.

Obviously this is tension-generating.

There are many things the ADD partner can do to improve. Multi-tasking – doing a second, more challenging task while executing a mundane one – helps a lot (listening to an engaging audiobook while doing laundry, for instance, improves that experience, so it is less likely to be forgotten). Fixed routines also help; when mornings include events in sequence – fix the coffee, walk the dog, prepare school lunches – then nested chores (take the trash out when it's full) become easier to include, when the routine causes the ADD partner to run right into them.

And it's important that the ADD partner take on those chores that are better-suited to ADD traits – those that require creativity, that are drumbeat-regular, or so simple that something else can be layered in.

For myself, my major contribution tends to be cooking. It's something I can hyperfocus on, from planning the menu to finding recipes to shopping to cooking to cleaning up – so I end up contributing considerably, never forget it's my job, and even look forward to it.

Every ADD adult can find similar roles that can make them a valuable contributor. It's a matter of working together to negotiate what those could be:

> "As you might guess, I'm not so great at chores. I forget to do things, and when my mind goes all pinball on me, I end up drifting off-task or doing a poor job. But I want to do my part, if you'll help me home in on those things I can do really well and keep in my mind. This might take some trial-and-error, but if you'll work with me to identify those things I can do to contribute, I'll do a great job!"

"What does 'perfect' mean?"

I met her for dinner, a couple of weeks after an ADD-fueled argument that had resulted in bad feelings. We were taking the first step toward working through it – not easy for either of us, but at least we were taking the step. It was, on balance, a happy meeting, and I enjoyed being with her again, though we only made a little progress that night.

But she did say one thing that really helped me understand what was happening and, in particular, how I was coming across.

"It's like you have this idea of 'perfection', when it comes to our relationship, and you're working to make that idea happen," she said, "and it seems to me that 'perfection' is something we work out together, over time."

Wow. She was so right, and I was so busted.

('Perfection', I hasten to add, does not in this case mean 'flawless', for which Zeus still waits; it means 'perfect for *us*'.)

I never intended to form that idea, or to mold my participation in our relationship in such a way as to bring it about. As I thought through what she'd said and reviewed our recent months together, I began to see another convergence of ADD traits: I was idealizing, while simultaneously avoiding confrontation and overpleasing.

And her proposal that we make the refinement of our relationship a joint project over time – no agenda, no schedule, no pressure – was as wonderful an invitation into the very best kind of relationship as anyone could hope for.

Is that what you want? Make it clear...

> "I don't want 'perfection' in our relationship
> to be something I fantasize and then pursue;
> I want it to be something we work out
> together over time..."

"Be my Whisperer?"

We can't do it alone.

And that's what many ADD adults do – they try to tough it out, they try to juggle all the burning bowling pins of ADD on their own. And they crash and burn, over and over.

We can't do it alone. We need help to get ourselves together and stay that way. We don't fully realize that it's that way for everyone, not just us: people need each other, people have to accept help in order to make life work as it should.

For me, this began many years ago, after my first divorce. At the time, I had never heard of ADHD and only vaguely realized that I was very different from most people. I tried to cover up my break-up as best I could. But I tumbled deep into dysphoria – the anxiety storm – and my best friend at the time, a fellow musician with whom I played in a band, tossed me over his shoulder and moved me into his home with his family.

And it was there that I experienced, for the first time, the one thing without which an ADD adult cannot make their way – someone who sees us as we really are, is willing to accept us that way, and will give us the help and encouragement we need.

I'm not talking about my musician friend here, though our friendship was truly life-changing in many ways; I'm talking about his wife, who saw beyond my anxiety storm and self-doubt, and gave me daily nudges to reach beyond my struggle and recover those things that gave me strength and energy – my commitment to my kids, my pride in my work, the music and the books that inspired me.

This was no casual thing. In hindsight, I realized that her patient support had not been incidental, but very intentional, even determined: she made a decision to commit time and effort to my healing, and it worked. She engaged me regularly in conversations that made me think. She exposed me to new ideas, which are my daily bread. She noticed and commented on every positive effort I made. My dysphoria ended, I began writing again, and I was able to begin the work of adapting to a new reality with my kids. When my ex came back not long after, wanting to reconcile, I was strong enough to say, 'I don't think that's best.'

I moved into my own place the following year, and my life proceeded. My musician friend and his wife divorced. It is no surprise that she became a very successful therapist.

Flash-forward more than 20 years: I've learned about my ADD, made significant life changes, done CBT. I experience a wonderful long-term relationship with a terrific woman, and she puts a name to that amazing gift I first experienced half a lifetime ago.

She calls herself *the Scott Whisperer*.

She knows about my ADD, even if she doesn't fully understand it, and she encourages me daily, keeping me focused, staying up to speed on each of my projects, smoothing over my moments of self-doubt. She asks questions about what I'm working on, what I'm thinking, what I'm studying. She brings an order and energy to my creativity and hyperfocus. And in the midst of this, she wisely cultivates fun and adventure for us to share.

A *Scott Whisperer*. My life went from a comfy amusement to a super-charged adventure. I became more productive and purposeful, by far, than I'd ever been.

She's no longer here, and that's on me – but she taught me how to make the most of my gifts, and the importance of having a whisperer in my life.

And I remembered my first whisperer, from long ago.

We've reconnected, and the years have only made what was good before that much better today. Now we are whisperers to one another.

Do you have a whisperer? Someone to give you daily encouragement, someone willing to work to understand those things that make you different, patient enough to walk alongside you when you're struggling? If you don't, make it a priority to seek out such a person:

> "You've been so patient, listening as I've described myself and my life! I want you to know how much I value your input and supportiveness. It would mean a lot to me if you'd keep it coming, and help me stay on track. Sometimes I don't have my priorities straight, and I'd appreciate you nudging me when I need it. Your encouragement means the world to me!"

"We can have an amazing sex life!"

Let's consider a very positive, encouraging fact about adult ADD: its various features can sometimes combine and work together to wonderful effect! Physical intimacy is one such area.

What are the ingredients of a really great sex life? Setting aside what *Cosmopolitan* might say, men and women generally agree on the big ones.

Connection: we flourish in physical intimacy when we feel a strong, deep, authentic connection with our lover;

Desire to please: we do best in bed when we are as interested in meeting our partner's needs as we are in having our own needs met;

Novelty: sex is best, and our bonds are strongest, when our bedroom life is filled not just with sexual relief, but with fun, creativity, and the sharing of new ideas.

If these three components are present in the bedroom, then all else is within reach: technique, frequency and other considerations are much more easily managed when this foundation is in place.

That said, often we start out with a new partner from a place of true disadvantage.

We ADD adults are not known for our self-confidence in general. And self-confidence is pretty important in the bedroom. Nor do we have a well-grounded sense of our own lovability, which can inhibit a connection that would otherwise blossom. In both cases, an ADD consequence that is not sex-specific can diminish our intimate experience with our partner, affecting our presence and our ability to bring to the moment what we truly wish to.

The ADD adult, then, could have strikes against them going in.

Another common bedroom issue for the ADD adult is the *initiation* of sex. The ADD partner wants sex, and is fully present when it occurs, but will not initiate.

The reason is obvious: ADD adults are hypersensitive to rejection. The problem is, this creates an issue for their partner.

Melissa Orlov, an expert on ADHD issues in marriage, tells of a wife who was frustrated with having to always be the one to initiate sex with her husband. This wife had "fallen into a classic ADHD relationship trap," Orlov wrote. "She [was] equating [her husband's] inability to initiate (an ADHD *symptom*) with his feelings for her. She has asked him to overcome his symptom in order to prove he loves her…yet the symptom *rules* here until such time as he identifies it as a symptom and puts specific behavioral habits in place (such as setting aside time in the calendar to plan a date at the instant he agrees with her that he will plan it). In order to succeed in changing this pattern, he needs a specific support structure that he doesn't currently have... In the meantime, he agrees he'll 'try harder' to remember to do this… and nothing changes, because his ADHD symptom remains unaddressed."

Cognitive Behavioral Therapy would help here. So would an ADD coach.

There are, then, two conversations here – one that takes place at the outset of a new relationship, and one to course-correct an out-of-balance relationship.

At the outset:

> "Being with you is going to be so much fun! I want our bedroom life to be filled with fun and excitement and creativity. If I seem to be holding back, it isn't you! It's my uneasiness about myself. I'll get over it quickly if we both commit to connecting and enjoying each other to the fullest. I'll be there, and I'll be really enthusiastic, if you can help me get there. I want to be a gift that you unwrap."

And where initiation is concerned:

"A problem I've had in the past is initiating sex. I want it very much, but I have trouble being the one to get things rolling. This has nothing to do with you at all! Or with sex either, for that matter – it's about my sensitivity to rejection. I take it too personally when someone tells me No. I'm working on that, and I really want to pull you into bed! But it might take me a while to get there. Can you be assured of my desire for you, and work with me on this?"

"Our life together can be a wonderful adventure!"

My last long-term relationship was *amazing*.

I'm a bookworm, as so many ADD adults are. I live for books, knowledge, new ideas. I have always had a deep fascination with the world, but well past 50, I still hadn't seen much of it. I was always happy with my books and music.

Then I fell in love with a woman who, to put it mildly, changed my life from top to bottom. It was, by far, the best relationship I'd ever been in, and she helped me arise from a life of self-satisfied amusement to a new and better life of true accomplishment, authentic faith in myself, courage to become more than I was, and an enthusiastic explorer of the world.

Across four years, we made trip after trip together. We saw both oceans. I went to a foreign country for the first time (not counting Canada). We spent weekends in cabins. We made repeated excursions into the Smoky Mountains to visit family. We went kayaking. We went on a cruise (my first). We visited endless bed-and-breakfasts. We hiked in the woods. We found a favorite creek and sat beside it often. We took in a Big Band evening. We stargazed. We saw the Grand Canyon (me for the first time). We saw dozens and dozens of movies in big-screen theaters (the ones with reclining seats that serve wine). We joined a wine club. We cultivated a close circle of friends and did fun things with them often (including some of the travel). We often took our kids with us. We tried new recipes. We took long walks.

I've never had so much fun in my life, and it awakened a part of me I didn't know existed. I'm still a bookworm, and I still love doing what I'm doing this minute – sitting at a keyboard, writing – but I'll never go back to the life I lived before she came into my world.[5]

My point: most ADD adults live largely in shadow, staying in safe zones, where the risk of being hurt or overwhelmed is minimal – just as I did for so long. We deny ourselves experiences like those above, not because we don't hunger for such things, but because they represent unknowns – and we are much more wary of unknowns than most people.

But it's my observation that we *do* hunger for such things! We are creatures whose minds thrive on the new-and-different, hungry for the novel and unusual, never more satisfied than when something unique is presented to us. The adventures that a couple can undertake together offer just this stimulation – a deeply satisfying journey for the ADD mind, before we even get to the wondrous effects that shared adventure can confer on the bond between two people who love each other.

It's not just healthy and stimulating. It can be transformative. It made me someone new, a different kind of man than I'd ever been before.

I hope this can be the experience of every ADD adult who feels drawn to it. Here are some words to introduce the idea to a new partner or friend:

"I want us to go to places we've never been, see things we've never seen, try things we've never done before! I want to explore the world with you, whether it's across the ocean or here in our own backyard. I want us to be Lewis and Clark, discovering wonders! I'm not very experienced at this, and you can bet I'll be hesitant at times, but not because I don't want to do it – I just feel some uneasiness when I'm faced with change. We can make this happen, together! What do you think?"

---

[5] If the reader wonders how I managed to lose such a partner, they need only observe that my new capacity for adventure still doesn't approach my capacity for saying the wrong thing at the wrong time. Dysphoria didn't help. Neither did red wine. I learned my lessons. The biggest one was, *Say the things in this book up-front...*

YOUR TAKE-HOME MESSAGE

"Despite everything, I don't regret my ADD – I love it!"

There are lots of pitfalls, obstructions, and challenges summarized in the preceding pages. The ADD life is a fierce undertaking, a daily struggle – too often, an endless parade of disappointment and loss and fatigue.

But it is also *wonderful*! Astonishing, fascinating - deeply gratifying in so many ways!

We ADD adults live lives that others cannot know – lives filled with gratifying accomplishment, marvelous surprises, and unexpected joy. Those superpowers of ours are magical! The assets of our character, forged in the fires of turmoil and heartbreak, have made us human beings of integrity and principle and empathy, well worth the love and respect of others.

I am decades into my life as an ADD adult, and I've long since accepted that I'm different. I no longer mind! I'm *proud* of my differences, I take delight in them. I spent so many years apologizing for who I am, and those days are over.

June Silny says it much better still:

> "Even though I have to deal with the
> rolling eyes of naysayers who think that
> I'm making up excuses, lies, and stories,
> I wouldn't change a thing in my brain.
> My ADHD allows me to love
> passionately, and to see color where
> others see black and white. I live outside
> the boxes and the lines. I fly without
> wings because amazing things do

happen. Change doesn't scare me. It
excites me. I embrace it. I see light in
the darkness. I can stay up all night
working on a project and deliver it the
next morning with an Oscar-worthy
performance. Some call it a burden, a
disorder, or a deficit; I don't think so. To
me it's a precious diamond that I need
to guard closely and polish often —
smoothing out the edges to discover
new sparkling dimensions every day.

"Give it up? No way! My ADHD is me.
It's in my heart and my soul. I love it that
way."

June speaks for me. Her words express exactly how I feel about my
ADD.

I read a story in an article about ADD not long ago that told of a young
Asian piano prodigy. She was a dazzling talent, attracting much positive
attention. In the midst of all this, she was diagnosed ADHD, and put on
meds. Her talents vanished.

The same thing happened to me. After I was diagnosed 15 years ago, I
took Strattera – and after a few weeks, my ability to write began to fade. I
switched to Concerta. No help.

There was no way I was giving up my hyperfocus. It was too much a
part of me. (It was also how I made my living, which was no small
consideration.) I gave up meds instead, and looked for other ways to
manage my ADD.

If you've read this far, it's very possible you feel the same way. Meds
or no, you have accepted your ADD as an essential part of you, not to be
tolerated or borne as a burden, but as a cornucopia of blessings.

If you feel this way, and if you've taken your partner/friend through the
various dialogs above - clarifying those traits, foibles, and strengths that
make you something unique and special - you'd do yourself an injustice if
you didn't express your embrace of your ADD and your satisfaction with
who it has made you.

You might say something like this:

"You've been so patient, letting me tell you about this part of me. But I want to say one more thing: even though ADD has its challenges, and sometimes makes my life truly difficult – I wouldn't trade it for anything! It lights my way, it fills me with wonder and energy, it is an endless flow of gifts. It is a source of unending beauty and adventure. I feel like it makes me special. I not only accept it, I celebrate it! I'm really hoping I can share this part of myself with you in a way that helps you appreciate it, too. I feel like we're going to share an incredible adventure!"

"Give me a chance..."

"Well, that's about it. I've shared a lot of myself in these conversations, and I'm so grateful for your willingness to listen. I guess we know each other pretty well after these talks, but there's still a lot to learn, and some it will be through (not altogether perfect experience.

"There are some things I can't promise you. I certainly can't promise I won't make mistakes; I can't promise that I won't embarrass you or myself at some point; I can't promise not to be exasperating, or that I won't try your patience more than once. In all fairness, though, wouldn't that be the case even if I didn't have ADD?

"Even so, there are tons of things I *can* promise! I can promise you that I'll give you the best I can, when I have it to give. I promise that I'll be open with you about my ADD, my feelings, my perceptions, and what's happening in my life. I'll be straight with you, and I expect the same: when you're annoyed or concerned or troubled by something I've said or done, I want you to speak up. I know those moments are going to happen.

"I can also promise you that what happens with us will be great fun, most of the time – and, on occasion, truly amazing! I'm hungry for adventure and excitement, and I want to be side by side when we find them. This will be a journey like no other!

"I can't fully express how difficult it is for me to say what I'm saying right now. ADD folks like me are fearless, when we take creative risks or adventurous risks or push ourselves to accomplish something that has seized our imaginations; but we are flat-out *terrified* of taking risks in relationships, because there are so few and they are so precious. It's costing me a lot to say all of this to you – and I realize how this must sound, and that this confession alone might push us apart.

"But it's worth the risk. I want to see what we can be. I want this time to be different, and I'm willing to go all-in to make it that way.

"Give me a chance!"

Afterword

I've already said that I wrote this book because I wish someone had
handed it to me years ago. Life would have been very different if I'd
learned about my ADD as a child, or if I'd understood dysphoria as a
young adult, known how to set expectations in a relationship, or known the
value of a whisperer early on. I'd have suffered far less frustration,
suffered far less self-doubt, suffered far less loss – I'd have suffered far
less.

We can't change yesterday, and today is what it is.

But we can change tomorrow.

The chapters of this book have already been field-tested in the private
ADD support community Uncommon Minds, on Facebook. And the
responses are very positive: the principle of expectation-setting early in
ADD relationships is one that shows a lot of promise.

It has certainly become my priority. Along with a personal commitment
I've made to transparency, openness about the things that make me who I
am and candid dialog with those I care about concerning the ways that I'm
different are my new normal. And I encourage anyone who's made it
through this book to give them a try.

We can't change yesterday, and today is what it is – but we can change
tomorrow.

Sources / Recommended Reading

Online sources

https://www.forbes.com/sites/carminegallo/2014/08/05/how-a-popular-tv-doc-has-learned-to-explain-adhd-simply/#654f86697da8

www.additudemag.com

https://www.ted.com/talks/jessica_mccabe_failing_at_normal_an_adhd_success_story/transcript?language=en

https://www.additudemag.com/slideshows/what-its-like-to-have-adhd/

Book sources

Beyond ADD: Hunting for Reasons in the Past & Present, Thom Hartmann. Underwood Books, 1996.

The Edison Gene: ADHD and the Gift of the Hunter Child, Thom Hartmann. Park Street Press, 2003.

The Gift of Adult ADD: How to Transform Your Challenges & Build on Your Strengths, Lara Honos-Webb, PhD. New Harbinger Publications, 2008.

The Edison Trait: Saving the Spirit of Your Noncomforming Child, Lucy Jo Palladino, PhD. Random House, 1997.

Journal articles

Fuermaier, A.B.M., Tucha, L., Koerts, J., Aschenbrenner, S., Weisbrod, M., Lange, K.W., & Tucha, O. (2013a). Source discrimination in adults with attention deficit hyperactivity disorder. PLoS ONE, 8(5), e65134.

Fuermaier, A.B.M., Tucha, L., Koerts, J., Aschenbrenner, S., Westermann, C., Weisbrod, M., Lange, K.W., & Tucha, O. (2013b). Complex prospective memory in adult patients with attention deficit hyperactivity disorder. PLoS ONE, 8(3), e58338.

About the author

Scott Robinson is a journalist, social scientist, healthcare consultant, public speaker and musician. He moderates an online ADD community, speaks to ADD groups and is certifying in cognitive behavioral therapy.